TALES IN A REARVIEW MIRROR

W/D

TALES IN A REARVIEW MIRROR

Donal Ruane

GILL & MACMILLAN

Gill & Macmillan Ltd
Hume Avenue, Park West, Dublin 12
with associated companies throughout the world
www.gillmacmillan.ie
© Donal Ruane 2003
0 7171 3596 9

Print origination by O'K Graphic Design, Dublin
Printed and bound by
Nørhaven Paperback A/S, Denmark

This book is typeset in 10/14pt Sabon.

The paper used in this book comes from the wood pulp of managed forests. For every tree felled, at least one tree is planted, thereby renewing natural resources.

A CIP catalogue record for this book is available
from the British Library.

5 4

For L. I hope business is booming.

Fly away on my Zephyr
I feel it more than ever
And in this perfect weather
We'll find a place together
Fly on … my wind.

The Zephyr Song
Red Hot Chili Peppers

Contents

Acknowledgements   ix

Prologue   1

"Taud I was in there"   7

"Fox-bleedin-rock, dat's wear"   15

Divorce on the N11   22

Jackie's Story   29

Have bike, will deal   40

The Runner   47

Romeo and Juliet   55

"Lucan, please"   63

Wayne, Texas Ranger   68

Fairytale of Dublin   79

"I dun nuttin!"   87

The Comedian   95

"How'm I supposed to get home?"   100

Poles Apart   111

Soiling Charges   119

The Menagerie   130

Lock up your daughters   138

Cops   145

Passport Control   150

Do you know who my daddy is?   157

Accounting for your movements   162

Two eggs in a hanky   167
Meeting   174
The Cider House Rules   180
Behind the Door   186
Takes two to tamango   196
Tactics   203
The S.M.B.W.I.T.W.   216
In de hite of it   225
The rules of attraction   233
Epilogue   240

Acknowledgements

This being my first book, varying degrees of indebtedness – in some cases quite literally – are owed to a number of people. I shall start with a very big thank you to my parents, one of them for vociferously encouraging me as I ventured into various fields which I had no experience of whatsoever, and the other for silently, and sometimes not so silently, steadfastly supporting me as I floundered in the long grasses of those same fields, all the time in hot pursuit of that most tantalisingly elusive of goals – an income without the bothersome constraints of a "career". Many thanks are also due to my four siblings and by now happily extended family for their continued support over the years, especially Noelie, whose character and generosity thankfully know no bounds. I must also thank my dozen or so good friends, for being just that. Thanks also to the good folk at Gill & Macmillan for getting behind this book so positively, and the people of Dublin for being its source material.

Prologue

Hi there. Thanks for buying the book. Or at least reading it. I suppose you could have borrowed it from a friend or something, which isn't really cool at all, because I won't have earned a royalty payment in that case. Or you could have stolen it, which is quite flattering really, given the potential consequences.

Anyway, I hope you enjoy it. It is what it is, no more and no less. I suppose looking back to when I was in college, I never thought that I would be driving a taxi at any stage in order to earn a living. I mean, driving a taxi in New York or Hong Kong is quite a cool way to earn a living. But Dublin? Nah. Too square. The people and lifestyles I mean, not the physicality of the city itself. But, all the same, now that I look bitterly back on the five years or so I have spent driving a taxi on and off around these increasingly mean streets, I have been an unwitting, sometimes partially witting, and once or twice very witting, party to some quite unusual incidents. Nothing terribly excessive really, which is unfortunate because I am quite voyeuristic and do like to see a bit of everything, but certainly such incidents could be justly classified as being beyond what most normal people would experience whilst driving around this shitty city.

Now, this is the prologue, the bit where I am completely

within my rights to take the opportunity to explain to you, the reader, some of the details about the book you have just bought, borrowed or stolen.

I won't keep you long here, don't worry. Suffice to say that I had meant to scribble down some of the more entertaining stories from my taxi-driving days for a long time before I actually got around to it, which was about a year ago. Not that I necessarily thought they would end up in a book such as this, though I privately held the view that they did indeed merit such recording and publication. No, it was more a therapeutic thing really. Though blessed with an excellent memory, I find that everyday life is filled with such clutter and trivia that even the most lucid of minds can sometimes forget those things that one would most like to remember. And then every so often, after regaling some friends with the details of yet another bizarre encounter, they would say, "Wow, you really are an unqualified genius. You should write a book." Well, not quite, but the book-writing suggestion bit is true. And so, here we are.

Now, a word or two about the way the book is written, the style in which it is written if you like (or lack of, depending on your opinion, which matters not a jot to me at this stage). I have a tendency to ramble on a little at times, to digress, to talk about many things at the same time, and indeed to talk about many things other than the thing I started off talking about. Bear with me. I'm sure you'll get used to it and maybe eventually acknowledge that it's part of what made reading the book so enjoyable. A conversational style I suppose you could call it, if one is being polite. If one wished to be impolite I suppose you could say that I'm possibly not that polished a writer. True, though I never claimed to be in the first place. Or that I fail to deal comprehensively and concisely with one topic before moving on to another. True as well perhaps, but it is *my* book, and if you're reading this now it means it got published, which is no mean feat. So there, you'll just have to put up with it.

Another thing you will notice about the book as you proceed is that I use the word "asshole" quite a lot. And for good reason too. It is, I feel, a very descriptive word. It can encapsulate a whole range of qualities about a person, and yet still sound reasonably inoffensive. The main point about this use of the word "asshole" is that I, the author of this *magnum opus*, would like to hereby assert that I am probably the biggest asshole I know, and that this manifests itself in all manner of actions and sayings.

Let's face it, I'm sure you have moments yourself when you act like a complete asshole. With your boyfriend, girlfriend, friends, family, partner, colleagues, parishioners, clients, patients, children, grandchildren, whoever. And there's nothing intrinsically wrong with that, as long as you recognise you're being an asshole, either during or after the action, publicly – or like myself, privately – and take some steps to reduce the frequency with which you are an asshole. So, the acknowledgement and consequent acceptance of my own quite alarming potential to be an asshole does, I think, give me a considerable head start on all the other assholes out there, simply because I *know* I'm an asshole. And that's quite something. Took me nearly a whole year to figure that one out, but now I know, and it's a good thing to know.

The reason I bring this up is because a reasonably large proportion of people (I actually typed "the vast majority of people" there first, but then, because I *know* I'm an asshole, I scaled it back to "a reasonably large proportion of people", which doesn't sound as ignorant or condescending at all. You see?) who get into my taxi are assholes. Some of them are complete assholes and probably act as such most of the time, and some, most really, may just be, for one reason or another, in asshole mode for the duration of our little trip. Whatever the case, I do enjoy observing these specimens in action, serving as it does, as a useful benchmark against which to measure my own propensity to be an asshole.

One thing most of these assholes have in common with each other, and indeed with the majority of people in this country, is their fondness of – or increasingly, their dependence on – alcohol as a social lubricant. As a result of our city fathers' laughable attempts to properly manage Dublin's infrastructure, I only work nights, and people using taxis at night do so primarily because they are pissed and need to get home. They say the truth comes out when people have drink on them and, though I usually avoid agreeing with clandestine factions with suspicious monikers such as "They", in this case I tend to agree with them, however sad an indictment on our nation's ability to be frank and honest that is. With my finely tuned observation skills I find that I can quite quickly pick up on a person's underlying character – especially when he or she is drunk – and would confidently say that in the space of our little ten or twenty minute trip I can accurately assess whether somebody is a decent sort of person or not. I can tell if they have an aggressive streak in them, or if they get moody, or if they're likely to hit their partner, what kind of father or mother they are, if they are happy young adults, that kind of thing. And to think I only get €1.80 a mile for this level of intuitive though silent analysis, and crack pot shrinks charge a hundred and fifty an hour for it!

So really, all I'm saying is that sometimes I do go on a bit and that a lot of the punters in my taxi are assholes. And as "they" say, it takes one to know one. So that's it, prologue over. Read on and see what you think.

P.S. Unfortunately, I had to change the names of all of the people featured in the following stories, some for their own sake, some for my sake, and some I just couldn't allude to in any way whatsoever. (Example: the currently serving member of the judiciary I collected from an outwardly seedy looking – though inwardly quite plush – private members club conveniently located near the Four Courts who got into my car extremely drunk and wearing little more than a tutu Shirley Temple would have been proud to call her own, once it had been taken in a little at the waist.) This was done under some duress, as I felt entitled to name and shame where I saw fit, but non-tutu-wearing legal counsel advised serious caution in this regard. Now, from the smattering of libel law I covered in college, I was under the impression that a rock solid defence in a libel case was the fact that the matter before the courts was true and therefore litigants could not claim they were libelled in the first place, but apparently our arcane legal system would side with the "injured" party all too easily, and that would not be cool at all, in that any royalties I might earn from the sale of this volume would be swallowed up in legal fees, and that wasn't the object of the exercise.

Believe it or not, I was initially advised not to use any names at all, but I strongly contested that on the grounds that I would then end up with a book full of "he said" and "she said" etc. etc. and such blandness would fly in the face of my undoubted literary talent. So in the end, it was agreed that I would change all names, and indeed some of the geography involved, in order to eliminate the possibility of some opportunistic bastard chancing his or her arm on a defamation action, claiming their reputation had been sullied and their life shattered, and that they felt "people were looking at them" and all that kind of shite, when in fact all they were doing was looking for a quick twenty grand settlement on the steps of the Four Courts. Regrettably, said location is becoming an increasingly congested place these days, if my solicitor's tales of the shenanigans taking place there are to be believed, and apart from the fact that he is a solicitor, I see no good reason not to believe him. So there you go, read on, and don't even think about it, or I'll screw you for everything you have in a counter claim.

"Taud I was in there"

Now we all know God loves a trier. But equally, one should be aware that He also hates a chancer. And all too frequently, said trier and chancer are in fact, one and the same asshole. So gentlemen, please bear this in mind as I recount the following cautionary tale.

It was a Thursday night, the week most of the offices were shutting down for Christmas. "Parties" all over the place. Normally nothing but grief, and invariably they end up diminishing the group cohesion they were supposed to strengthen. I'm sure some of them have a good time together, it's just that at Christmas I always seem to get the saps who didn't, and it's such a complete pain in the arse. Bitch, bitch, bitch, all the way home. About their job and their colleagues. Did I ask them to sit in some poxy cubicle and answer phone call after phone call all day, reading from a script prepared by Bob Lipinski, Senior VP Customer Relations, over in Albuquerque? No, I didn't. Is it my fault that nearly everyone they work with is an under-achieving Trinners asshole just back from Australia who will not shut the fuck up about how cool Sydney is? No it isn't, so why burden me with the shortcomings of your crappy life?

Anyway, through the lights at Harcourt Street and on to the green. Big queue at the rank, the way I like it. I always slow down to a crawl as I near the front of the queue so I can check out what kind of moron I am going to get in the back of the car. If they look particularly messy I either pull off again and go around the corner to Habitat and pick up some eternally grateful punter who would otherwise have been spirited away by some thieving hackney bastard, or I stop just short of the aforementioned excessively messy bastard and let the next person in the queue get in and then pull off quickly before his alcoholically-depleted quintet of brain cells click into gear and he starts shouting obscenities at me before starting a fight with anyone who looks sideways at him.

And there he is. A bloke, about twenty-seven or twenty-eight. Let's call him Alan. Pissed, of course. Stuffing the last of his kebab into his gob, careful not to get any entrails-of-cat-in-sheep-shit-sauce on his fetching M&S matching shirt and tie set, inwardly cursing the "lezzer" in Break for the Border who defied both human logic and her own irrefutable inner desires and elected not to go home with him and have the worst sex of her life in a smelly bedroom which said ape shared with JP from Meath who snored like a rhino farting as he slept in his sweat-stained GAA club jersey on the other side of the room.

There was a painfully fashionable south county darling standing in the queue next to Alan. Well, I say next to, but really she was trying to remain outside the arc of his drunken spiral whilst at the same time not allowing anyone else to usurp her position in the queue. Deducing that Alan's inebriation and more than likely imbecilic nature would not relegate him any further down the food chain than any other potential clients that night, I stopped about six feet in front of him and looked in the rearview mirror. He was chatting away to Lady Penelope of Silchester, trying to get her into the taxi. Unbelievable neck on the guy.

(His antics reminded me of a guy I used to know a couple of years ago. This guy could not gallantly accept that some nights, and in his case most nights, he simply was not going to score. He would have his list of hot spots lined up, and with a display of discipline, zeal and dogged determination that was terrifyingly absent from his professional life, would systematically proceed from one pub to another in search of a "bird", refusing to call it a day, or a night as it were, until all avenues of potential amorous liaison had been explored in full. His spirit only broke at roughly the same time as the dawn of a new day. No stone was left unturned, and scarily, sometimes, under the very last stone – the taxi rank – he would strike gold, or at least bronze in the context of the women he would end up with. I recall one particular Sunday afternoon when he took great pleasure in telling me that he had "clicked with a lovely birdie" whilst in the throngs of the taxi rank on Dame Street at four o'clock that morning. Something of a double whammy for this particularly tight bastard, as she lived near him and they could split the bloody fare!)

So there's Alan, obviously trying the same approach with this girl.

"No, seriously. Ye can share this with me if you like, save ye standing around here all night. Ye know yourself what taxis are like at Christmas, the shower of bastards."

Lady Penelope of Silchester had to weigh this one up. Share a taxi home with this drunken sap and endure the relentless babbling or stand at the rank and wait for the next member of said "shower of bastards" to grace her with their presence?

"But I live in Blackrock."

The "but" was there to infer to Alan that, given his unsightly demeanour, the proposed taxi-sharing was impractical in that he couldn't possibly live anywhere near her.

"No bodder, sure it's on the way."

Cursing her decisions firstly, not to bring a jacket with her that night, and secondly for being led astray by those bimbos in *Sex and the City* and believing that shoes that looked *this* good could also be comfortable, Lady Penelope capitulated and smiled faintly at Alan.

"Oh, Okay. Thanks."

Whether it was through a rare moment of chivalry or just a delayed reaction from the alcohol, Alan held open the door to his lair for the young princess. In she gets, scuttling over to the far side of the back seat, followed quickly by Prince Charming.

"All right, boss? Blackrock, please."

"No problem," I say, settling back to enjoy the spectacle he was surely to make of himself. No mention of his own destination yet. Obviously waiting to see how well he gets on with the young lady before throwing the towel in.

"So, what's yer name then?" he asks.

"Em, Sarah," Sarah said (obviously).

"Very nice te meet you Sarah. I'm Alan."

The year in finishing school in Switzerland paying rich dividends, Sarah politely extends her manicured hand in reciprocation of Alan's proffered mit.

"Alan. Hi. Oh, thanks for the lift by the way."

"Not at all, sure it's bloody freezin' out there. Couldn't leave ye standing there all night. At a party were ye? Office do, yeah?"

"Not so much an office thing. Clients bringing us out for dinner."

"Dinner, yeah? Very nice, very nice. Where'd ye go?"

"Ah, The Unicorn?"

Alan shakes his head as though he'd just missed out on the conundrum on Countdown.

"No, sorry, don't know it. Any good is it?"

Sarah recoils momentarily at his ignorance of the Dublin gastronomic scene, but keeps the conversation going in a terrifically sporting fashion.

"Oh God, yeah. Really good food, and great wine."

Just sitting at the lights at Jury's in Ballsbridge now. Time was ticking away, but now Alan was back on familiar territory.

"Oh yeah? Gettin' stuck in to the vino! I like it! Locked are ye?"

"Sort of, dreading getting up in the morning!"

"Bollocks te that, I'm not goin' in. Why don't ye pull a sickie?"

Sarah pauses for a moment, fantasising about ringing in sick and staying in bed all day, then snaps out of it, disgusted at her sudden lapse of character.

"God no, that wouldn't go down well at all."

"Fair enough. Well I've no intention of goin' in, told me boss that tonight as I was leavin' too."

I kind of got the feeling that Alan wouldn't be missed too much at work the following day, and that some time in the not too distant future, at a performance review, he might be informed that far from missing him, the company had made steady progress without him and had decided to dispense with his services altogether. Sarah allows herself a little tipsy titter at this feral boy's feckless attitude.

"Good for you! And what were you up to?"

Big mistake, Sarah. Mentioning the word "you" twice in such a short space of time to a moron like Alan. With what's on his mind probably the only thing that's *ever* on his mind, that's like a red rag to a bull. And a horny bull at that. "She likes me," Alan's thinking. *Wants to know all about me and what I was doing tonight. This is going deadly!*

"Out with the gang from the office. Christmas do in Break for the Border, ye know?"

"Really? Good fun, I presume?" Sarah enquired politely.

"Ah, yeah it was alright, I suppose. Wasn't much in the way of free gargle, mind. Boss is a bit of a sap, ye know? Tight as a duck's arse. Bleedin' Christmas an' all!"

"God yeah," said Sarah, "you'd think they'd look after you for one night."

"Exxacly, one night of the year, wouldn't kill them. And you wanna have seen him on the dance floor, givin' it socks he was! Taud 'e was only deadly!"

"Oh God, sounds awful."

A lull in the proceedings. Alan looks out at the unfamiliar surroundings of the Merrion Road and tries to assess how far it is to Blackrock. He straightens himself up and slides towards the centre of the seat.

"So eh, have you all your shopping done?"

"God, no, not a bit. I'm *so* last minute, it's crazy."

Sarah makes a mental note to go in to BT's that Saturday with her VBF Rebecca and do her shopping, courtesy of daddy's gold card. It's the thought that counts, after all. Alan seizes the opportunity to do a little digging.

"And eh, have you got someone special to buy for?" Alan probed, ever so indelicately.

Sarah smiles politely and shakes her head.

"Em, no. I haven't got time for that right now, what with work and college and everything."

She could just as easily have held up the aforementioned red rag and started waving it flirtatiously in front of Alan's eyes.

"Oh now, don't start, sure ye have te have a bit o' crack. Life's too short te be working all the time, ye know?"

"Yeah, I know, I just want to get my exams out of the way first."

"And when are dey over?"

Jesus, subtle or what? Alan does the old cinema routine, resting his outstretched arm on the back of the seat. Sarah, convent school innocent that she is, doesn't immediately register his Lothario-like instincts.

"Not until summer I'm afraid. We've a break for Christmas though, which is great, forget all about it for a while. I'm actually off to Galway for Christmas. The whole family get together down there with relatives."

"Oh yeah, wen are ye off?" enquires Alan, trying to work out how much time he has to complete his conquest, deluding himself into thinking that he might actually see this girl again if, sorry when, tonight's endeavours come to nothing.

"Mum and Dad are already down there, took off early to relax for a few days. I'm going down with my brothers at the weekend."

Free gaf! Alan can't believe his ears and is sure that it is now game on. He tries to contain himself as we near the Blackrock shopping centre. I figure that this is as good a time as any to intervene to ask directions.

"Whereabouts in Blackrock do you want?"

Alan shoots me a scornful look, as if I had callously betrayed some previous agreement we had where I would drive all the way to Delgany if necessary so he could pursue his quest.

"Oh, sorry, I'm off Carysfort Avenue. Do you know it?"

"Yeah I do, grand."

No right turn off the by-pass on to Carysfort so I swing in to the village to go straight through the lights. The clock is ticking now, as well as the meter. Alan's under pressure to close the deal, and in a deliberate effort to thwart his advances, I tear up Carysfort Avenue, screeching to a halt when Sarah says, "Here on the left is fine, thank you."

She sits up, somewhat relieved to be home. Alan sits up and get out his wallet.

"How much is dat?" he says.

Sarah looks perplexed.

"I'm sorry?"

Alan adopts a hurt, betrayed look.

"I taud we might ..."

"I don't think so. My God, what a nerve! Here's some money towards the fare. Goodnight, and a very happy Christmas."

She throws him a tenner, gets out and slams the door, instantly sobered and chastened.

Alan shakes his head, trying to figure out how he could have misread the signals. I gave him a minute to regroup.

"And where are you heading for?"

"What? Oh yeah, sorry. Where are we?" he asked, somewhat dazed by the red card just issued to him.

"Blackrock. Where are you off to?"

"Blackrock? Ah bollocks, how far is it te Killester?"

"About twenty quid," I said, trying not to laugh out loud.

"Fuck it, taud I was in there."

"Fox-bleedin-rock, dat's wear"

Middle of the week and not much happening. I was shooting down Thomas Street, heading back towards the centre. Two slappers tottering along in their stilettos turn and wave frantically at me. The way they wave me down bugs the shit out of me, and I'm tempted to keep going but it's a slow night and there's bills to be paid. Instead of standing patiently at the kerbside and raising their right arm aloft as one should when hailing a taxi, they keep walking, half turned in my direction and flap their hands up and down in a pathetic motion, as though they were both drunkenly slapping eight-year-old boys on the head. It's a gesture used quite frequently by people hailing a taxi and it really annoys me, not just because it looks moronic, but because it reminds me of a particular incident that happened a good while ago, an incident so disturbing it still lingered clearly in my mind.

It was early on a Sunday evening. Things were quiet enough, so I was touring around the suburbs looking for a fare. Rolled around a corner at the Dodder Park, heading along by the riverbank. And there he is, the world's greatest dad, moral custodian of the neighbourhood, honorary chairman of the Rathfarnham chapter of the Guardian Angels, okely-dokely Ned Flanders himself, out enjoying the warm evening with his son. Little brat must have been at least six and still hadn't mastered the art of cycling on two wheels. No, this kid had about sixteen stabilisers on his trike, and still couldn't propel himself along the footpath in a straight line. Probably something to do with the intra venous slush puppy drip he was towing along behind him.

Anyway, the kid starts veering towards the edge of the footpath. Being the masterful driver I am, I had the situation clocked and took evasive action, manoeuvring casually out over the line into the oncoming lane, which happily contained no oncoming traffic, thereby giving the little brat plenty of room to fall off his trike and cut himself to shreds on the tarmac. A precautionary measure. No big deal, no "incident" to report, thanks to my observation and anticipation. But Ned Flanders doesn't see it this way. No, he sees me coming – wilfully driving a mechanically propelled vehicle along a public thoroughfare – and, recalling Clint Eastwood's performance in *In the Line of Fire*, hurls himself in front of his lard ass son's trike to protect him from the crazed sociopath driving the dangerous car-like car, glad to take the proverbial bullet, but secretly hoping that it'll just be a flesh wound and he'll live to recount the gory tale over tea and battenburg slices at the next residents association meeting where his motion to petition the council for speed ramps to be laid every five metres along that same dangerous stretch of road is unanimously carried. Complete and utter asshole.

I shake my head forlornly at his pathetic antics and go merrily on my way, glancing in the rear–view mirror as I do so. And there he is, weeping with gratitude that his gormless kid was spared by the good Lord from being deliberately crushed by my Panzer-like

Toyota Corolla, and waving his floppy hand up and down, imploring me to slow down before I lose control of my vehicle – which must have been doing at least thirty miles an hour – and career on to the footpath, mowing down an overweight kid and his hapless father, when, in reality, my skilful manoeuvre was in fact a vehicular acknowledgement of same fat kid's inability to ride a trike in a straight line along a footpath wide enough to land a 747 on. It was me, as a professional driver, signalling by my actions that I was aware of the slight possibility that the little shit could end up on the road and that I was taking steps to ensure that, were this to happen, there would be no collision and/or fatality.

The guy was such a moron, I was seriously tempted to turn around, go back and chew the face off him, slashing the tube on little Rod's IV drip as I left. But I didn't, figuring that there would be no reasoning with an asshole of that magnitude.

So that's why I don't like people waving me down in such a fashion. Anyway, big deep sigh and I pull over. In they get, one in the front and one in the back. Absolute brazzers. Mid-twenties, bet into their Ilac Centre clothes – thought they were only gorgeous. Hair coloured from the contents of a family sized bottle of bleach, which they probably emptied, and make-up from a five-litres-for-the-price-of-four tub from the Cat-from-Eastenders "Sofistikated" line.

The one in the front leads the discussions.

"Alrigh'? We're just goin' over te Cork Stree', de Swan, yeh?"

"No problem," I said, waiting for the follow-up. Things are never that simple with this lot. Always something extra to do en route – score some drugs, wait for a Chinese, collect kids, drop off a babysitter, there's always something.

Then her mate fills me in on the details.

"Haf te stop off in de Spar mister. Haf to get a pair of bleedin'

17

tites, me legs are freezin'. Alrigh'?"

"Fer fucks sake Sharin, what's up wit ye? Yer grand, we'll be dere in a minit."

"Bollix Trace, I'm not goin' in dere like dis, bleedin' stait o' me. I'll owney be a sekind."

Echoing my sentiments exactly, if not grammatically or phonetically, "Trace" responds with, "Ye bleedin' dope, dere's all wis sumtin' wrong wit ye!"

I pull up outside the Spar and Sharon gets out. Tracey takes the opportunity to light up a smoke. After taking a drag, she holds the cigarette up to me and says, "Alrigh' yeh?" I nod affirmatively, deducing that it would be a waste of time and energy to inform her that she was actually in breach of regulations recently set down in statute. Some ash falls onto her surprisingly expensive looking leather jacket.

"Bollix!" she says, wiping it to the floor.

"D'ye like me jacket?"

"Yeah, it's cool," I said, trying to contain myself from the overwhelming desire I had to examine the intricate stitching and beautiful texture of said leather coat.

"Eigh' hundrid pound dat cost, righ?" she says, sticking her sleeve in front of my face for examination. "Eigh hundrid pound, an' I'm still goin' out on a Wensdey nite."

"Fair play," I respond, kind of half meaning it, marvelling at her fiscal rectitude.

"I want fer nuttin, righ?"

She pauses to take a satisfied pull on her cigarette, staring straight out the front window as she does so.

"Me fella done a job dere a while back. Robbed a jeep fer a job. Took de rap, got sent down fer it. New he wood an' all like, but he got looked after well, d'ye know whad I mean?"

Back to Tracey. She's still looking out the window, as though she were talking to herself. I sit there and let her rabbit on. Meter's ticking, I'm happy enough. God knows what's keeping Sharon – she's obviously not satisfied with the range of denier available at the Bic hosiery concession in the Spar shop, and is letting everyone know it.

"So we got our money, and baut a house. Fuckin' deadly it is too. An' wen he gets out, dat's it, we're all sed up."

I had a made a nice few bob in the property market over the previous couple of years (and then unwisely pissed it away producing a feature film), and retained a strong interest in property matters, so my curiosity was aroused with the mention of her acquisition.

"Oh yeah? Where did you buy the house?" I asked.

She looks at me, smug grin on her face, and says, "Fox-bleedin-rock, dat's wear."

Trying to contain a fit of laughter, I nodded my head slowly as I regained my composure.

"Foxrock, yeah?"

She then tells me where she bought the house, the road name and the number. She could have been full of shit and just picked them both out of thin air, but I was intrigued as to why, if her story was bullshit, she bothered with the specifics. It was a measure plainly out of keeping with her otherwise imbecilic nature, so I made a mental note of the details.

"Very nice. When did you do that?" I continued.

"Signed de contracts las week. Gonna pay fer it in cash an' all," she said triumphantly.

I should bloody well hope so. The thoughts of a scrubber like her getting loan approval for a three hundred grand house while she and her extended family of ingrates bleed the state dry for every category of assistance under the sun would not do much for one's confidence in the national banking system, frail as it already is.

Tracey smokes the last of her cigarette as Sharon gets back in the car, slamming the door as she does so.

"Bleedin' kip!"

"'Bout bleedin' time an' all, Sharin! What de fuck were ye doin? Makin' de bleedin' tings?"

"Relax de kax, Trace, we've loads o' time. Dey didden have de ones I wanted. Lite us a smoke wile I put dese on."

As I drive down Francis Street heading for the aforementioned hostelry, Sharon proceeds to pull off her boots, open the pack of tights and unfurl them up each leg, thrusting her crotch skyward as she stretches them around her fat arse and under the waistband of her skirt. After attending to the details, she plonks a leg in between the front seats, jiggling her toes in Tracey's direction.

"Dey alrigh Trace?"

"Jaysus Sharin! Dey're grand, now get yer smelly fuckin' feet outta me site!"

"What's up wit yew?"

"Dere's nuttin' up wit me, I just don't want yer smelly feet in me face, alrigh'?"

Sharon disconsolately puts on her boots and fixes her hair, reaching over my shoulder to adjust the rearview mirror as she does so. When satisfied that she is indeed the belle of the ball, she languishes amorously across the back seat, mistakenly confident in the knowledge that I, like any other heterosexual hot-blooded male would surely find her devastatingly attractive and consequently ply her with Bacardi Breezers all night in the hope of shagging her in the living room of her mother's council house, restraining my shrieks of admiration at her sexual prowess lest we wake her infant child.

"Hey, Trace, d'y reckin Anto'll be here tonigh?"

"Cudden care less if 'e is or not."

"Yeh righ! Sniffin' around after yew las Saterdey nite he was, an' yew were lovin' it!"

"I was in me hole! Shut yer bleedin' mouth Trace or I'll burst ye."

I pull up across the road from the pub and tally the meter. Sharon shoots me a scornful look.

"Jaysus, swing around will ye? It's freezin'."

Bone lazy they are, wouldn't walk across the road for a job. Swing the car around and say, "Now girls, that's €7.40 please."

Sharon recoils in horror. "Seven forty? Me bollix! We owney went 'round de bleedin' corner!"

Tracey intervenes diplomatically, thrusting a tenner nonchalantly at me.

"Dere ye are, keep de change. Tanks."

"Cheers. All the best", I say, more than content with the generous gratuity. As far as I'm concerned, her money is as good as anyone else's, whether it be the proceeds of very well organised crime or not.

Out they get and into the pub. I go on my merry way and work away for the rest of the night. About two in the morning I'm dropping an account customer home to Deansgrange when I recall the emphatic and geographically concise details of Tracey's alleged acquisition. I leave your man home and get out the map to find the exact location of the road she mentioned. Only a minute away, so I swing over to have a look. I'm cruising down the road straining to see which way the numbers go, when I notice an estate agent's hoarding in the garden of a house. No. It couldn't be. Yes. It is. The right house number, and a "Sale Agreed" board tacked to the bottom of the sign.

God help the neighbours.

Divorce on the N11

This particular trip is memorable in that it was far and away the most extreme domestic I have encountered. Now, domestics, as the name implies, normally do, and in my opinion always should, arise and be resolved within the cosy confines of one's own abode. But this one couldn't wait, no way.

Now, rows in a taxi are nothing new and they generally focus on the areas of alleged infidelity, the prowess or otherwise of amateur or professional sportspeople, and the success or otherwise of one or more persons present in the car in their efforts at attracting the opposite sex. A common factor in most of these exchanges is the presence of alcohol in the bloodstreams of all concerned, and is no doubt commonly used as mitigating circumstances the day after for any hurt or offence caused to another party during the disagreement in question. And in fairness to those concerned, by and large, no harm is meant in the outbursts that usually occur, but this particular incident was choc full of malice, and deliberately so.

It was a Friday night, around one in the morning. Things were hotting up nicely and I was whipping out through Donnybrook heading for the Montrose hotel. As I passed Bective I saw a few bodies in black tie floating around and made a mental note to come back that way. Normally at this time on a Friday and Saturday night I would work my way out towards Blackrock and Dun Laoghaire and stay around there for the night. Lots of local hops around the south county instead of town to Lucan, back in empty, town to Swords, back in empty, that kind of shit. I always found it handy enough out around the south county – less ramps, less cops, and generally you're dealing with a better class of asshole. So I drop off at the hotel, swing across the flyover and shoot back down to Donnybrook. This chap in a tux waves me down and I pull in outside the Shell garage. He strolls across the road and opens the door, turning impatiently in the direction of his better half, gesturing at her to hurry up.

"We're going to Bray please, if my fucking wife would ever grace us with her presence."

Not good, didn't like the sound of this at all. A tallish slender woman, mid-thirties with short blond hair, hops across the road through the traffic and gets in the back. Asshole slams the door and gets in the other side, remembering to slam that door as well, then barks the instructions at me.

"Bray please, first exit off the motorway. I'll show you where to go."

Bray at one in the morning. What a complete pain in the arse. I was actually living there at the time and such a fare at four or five in the morning when I was looking to finish up would have been sweet, but at this time it kind of threw things out of whack. Still, that's the way it goes so I get out the short country fare list and pretend to check what the damage is out to Bray. Thirty-five fifty from the city centre, but I make an allowance for the fact that we're already in Donnybrook.

"It's €35 out to Bray, alright?"

"Fine. That's fine."

Now, this couple, who we'll call Jack and Jill for the crack, were obviously in the middle of a serious row, and I hadn't even got to the Montrose when it all flared up again after a short recess, which had given asshole Jack an opportunity to practise his sighs and snorts, which even then were nowhere near the quality I can achieve when the situation calls for it, and quite often even when the situation doesn't particularly call for it.

"I'm sorry Jack, I just didn't look at it when he gave it back to me ..." Jill said.

"Yeah Jill, you just didn't look at it. A fucking scumbag taxi driver takes a fifty off me to take you home to Bray, then decides he can't go and gives you back a tenner! Jesus wept!"

"Look, he could have made a mistake. You don't know ..."

"I *know* he's a fucking scumbag. He knew exactly what he was doing," the husband interrupted.

Absolutely no consideration for my feelings as a taxi driver, I have to point out. The wife was quite right, it could have been a mistake, but as far as the facts of the situation were concerned, I would have to go along with her asshole husband: the taxi driver in question was probably a scumbag. Your man hails the taxi and gives the guy a fifty to take his wife home. She gets in the back, they go twenty yards down the road and the driver pretends he's got a call on the radio and can't go to Bray and gives her back the money, knowing she won't argue because she's a polite, reserved woman. She takes the note, gets out and walks back to her husband. He's pissed off at the sight of her, having hoped to slip back in to the do and go on the lash with all the rugger buggers, and then totally flips when he sees the con job the guy is after pulling. Hails a taxi again – me – and drags her home himself. Now fair enough, you'd be pissed off at being down forty euro, but you can't take it out on the other half, it's not like she was a

24

willing accomplice in the scam and was planning to meet up later on with the taxi driver at the airport to abscond to Rio with the forty euro! But he was really making her suffer, the sap. He was fairly well on at this stage anyway, and I'd say that this latest episode was just something he was using to have a go at her.

"All I know is that I felt ill and had to leave. I didn't ask you to leave with me, so don't take it out on me that you missed out on your great night out," she continued.

"For fuck's sake Jill, you couldn't even manage to get a taxi on your own. I hadn't got much choice now, had I?" asshole countered with.

This was no hushed disagreement with a just-you-wait-till-I-get-you-home undertone. No, this was full on, raised voices, the whole kit and caboodle. The wife tried to continue with her line of reasoning.

"You didn't have to come with me, so stop being so nasty. I could have got a taxi up to my parents' house and Dad would quite happily have paid the taxi driver and dropped me home ..."

"Oh yeah, sure, you arrive at your parents' house at one in the fucking morning on your own with no money? That's great ammunition for them, and then I'm the biggest wanker in the world. That's all I need."

"What are you talking about ammunition? They're my parents, Jack. They would have given me the money for the taxi and driven me home, that's all I'm saying."

"Yeah Jill, sure, whatever you say," he said disdainfully.

This guy was seriously bugging me, he was such an asshole, treating his wife like this. I don't excuse this kind of thing on the grounds that he was half pissed at all. This was the way he really was under the veneer of respectability he displayed at work or in the company of others. This was the man she had married, and if I knew it, then she knew it, and that must have felt so crap.

By this stage I'm through the lights at Cabinteely and I'm shooting along trying to get to Bray asap. I want these people out of my car before this thing really explodes. Asshole is staring out the window, immune to the sobs emanating from his wife. He reaches into his jacket, looking for something.

"Fuck it, now I've lost my cigarettes. Pull into the Esso here. I have to get cigarettes."

Please, thank you, you're welcome. I say nothing and pull in to the garage. He gets out and reluctantly takes his rightful place in the queue. Jill takes out a tissue and wipes her eyes.

"I am so sorry about this, I really am," she says to me. "This is so embarrassing, arguing like this in your car. I don't know what's come over him ... He's only like this when he's drunk ..."

"He's a complete asshole if you ask me. Do you want me to take you to your parents' house? We'll leave him here to walk home. Might straighten him out a bit," I said, turning around to squeeze her hand and give her a smile.

Not really my policy to intervene in these types of situations at all, but I honestly hadn't come across one as nasty as this before. The venomous way he spoke to her freaked me out. If I ever heard anyone talking to a woman I knew like that I'd deck the bastard, or at least try to.

"Oh God no, I couldn't do that," Jill said, trying to return my well intentioned smile, "he'd go mad."

"That's the idea. You stay with your parents tonight, let him walk home and cool off."

"No, honestly, it'll be fine. I know what has to be done," she said, straightening herself up as asshole approached the car. He gets in and, true to form, slams the door.

"Fucking idiots, can't understand a simple request," he barks, reaching forward to the front passenger seat. For a second I thought he had seen me talking to his wife and was going to whack me for interfering, but he just flung some money down on the seat and slumped back against the door, as far away as possible from his wife.

I moved off quickly and headed for the motorway. After a minute, Jill clears her throat and calmly says, "Tomorrow morning we are going to go over this one more time, Jack. You seem to think I'm being irrational in some way or that I'm not all there or something, but let me tell you that I am perfectly in control of my senses, and it's you that has the problem ..."

"Jill, don't start this shit again, I'm tired of it. I just want to ..."

"Excuse me, I'm not finished. You seem to have a problem with me, and our marriage. We will discuss it and if there is no resolution, then you can have your divorce, because I am not going to live my life this way."

"Oh Jesus, don't be so dramatic Jill ..."

"I am not being dramatic, I am facing up to the reality of the situation. I will not be made to feel like there is something wrong with me and that everything is my fault. I would much rather be alone than live with you if this is the way you are going to treat me."

Well said darling. Not a pip out of asshole now. I was smiling as I turned up the road he had stipulated. I swung into the estate and followed the directions to their house. I pull up at the kerb, asshole gets out and guess what, he slams the door. The wife gets out and lets him walk up the driveway before turning to me. I know it might sound corny, but she seemed stronger somehow, determined to change the way things were. I'm not suggesting for a second that my little bit of marriage guidance counselling had anything whatsoever to do with it. I'm sure it was simply the realisation on her part that she was married to an asshole and that life didn't have to be like that.

"I am sorry you had to witness all that," she said to me. "It can't have been very pleasant, and I apologise for the way he spoke about your colleagues. I know it's not an easy job you do, and that the vast majority of you are decent people ..."

"Look, don't worry about me," I said. "Look after yourself and remember tonight tomorrow morning. Take care."

She smiled and nodded her head.

"Oh I will, don't worry. Good night."

She turned and headed towards her unhappy home, where asshole had politely left the door open after him. I waited until she got in, swung the car around and headed off, lighting a much-needed cigarette as I hit the motorway. After that episode I needed some good time party people in the car, so I headed up to Club 92 to see what was happening. Couldn't get two like that in a row.

Jackie's Story

aturday night of the August bank holiday weekend, and there's not a sinner on the streets. Not only have the culchies gone home to mammy with the washing, but thousands of city folk have decided to join them and get pissed in Galway or Kilkenny for a change. About ten o'clock I decide it's time for some comfort food and head for Spar on Baggot Street. I jostle my way through the hordes of my brethren standing around outside with their coffee and cigarettes as they verbally right the wrongs of the world we live in. I grab a bottle of Coke and head for the counter, and, succumbing to the attractive merchandising of the confectionery products, grab not one, but two bars of chocolate. I am just about to hand over the money when a fellow driver charges into the shop and shouts, "Who's 8064? Who's 8064? They're lifin' ye!"

The number registers with me, as it should, seeing as how it's my plate number. I leave the goods behind and leg it out of the store to see that there is a tow truck parked parallel to my taxi, beside which are two lads fastening lifting cables to the car. I was parked at the bus stop, fair enough, but I wasn't in the shop a full minute before they pounced. I declared their behaviour draconian and heavy handed and demanded they release my car, but to no avail. Up she goes and off to the pound. A number of taxi lads then come over and explain to me that if I had got back into the car and refused to move, they couldn't have lifted it, and would eventually have had to release it. As anyone interested in the art of deliberate stock price manipulation knows, the value of a certain piece of information is directly related to its timeliness, but I thought it futile to go into this with them at that point in time. Nothing for it, had to get a bloody taxi down to the pound and pay €160 to get it released.

The night was going to be a complete washout at this rate – down €160 before I'd even covered my petrol money. Decided to go up to the Maxol in Harold's Cross to finally purchase my by now much needed comfort food. Over the canal and up the road I go. As I near the park I see a girl standing on the other side of the road waiting for a taxi. Then I see an empty taxi coming down past the dog track and assume he'll get to her before I can swing around. But then his lights begin to change, and like an idiot, he slows down to stop instead of speeding up to get through them and get the fare. So for the crack, I decide to see if I can get the fare ahead of him and tear up the side of the park past him, hang a right at the bike shop, and a right again at the Inn on the Park. Seeing as how everybody's in Galway, there's no traffic so I get around the park dead handy. I then tear down the other side of it and sail through the amber-tinted green light and promptly stop at the beckoning punter. An emphatic victory.

"Did you jus' go past me a sekind ago?"

"I did yeah."

"Ah, yer very good."

"Not really. I was heading for the shop and then decided to see if I could beat the other lad to you. Where're you off to?"

She hasn't actually got in the car yet. She has the side door open and is leaning in whilst talking to me. From the other side of the road, she had looked fairly hip and kind of cute, but faraway fields and all that, she was actually a lot older and somewhat bedraggled looking. A working girl if I'm not mistaken.

"Listen, will ye do me a favour? I'm goin' down te work, but I have te go down te Fatima furst, yeah? I've owney six euros on me, but I'll sort ye out later on. Ye can come down te me and I'll give ye de rest, yeah?"

She seemed sound enough, and I'd kind of written off the night anyway, so what the hell, I nodded in agreement. She smiles and gets in.

"Tanks a million. Yer a star. Can I borrow yer fone fer a minit?"

"Jesus, no money, no phone, you're pushing it now, aren't you?" I said.

"Yeah, well I had a dodgy punter de udder nigh', had te ged out of 'is car quick at de lights, an' it fell outta me purse. I'll owney be a sekind, jus' hafte sort out sumtin."

I hand her my phone and as she calls her dealer I pull into the Shell garage on Parnell Road to await the results of the negotiations.

"Dave, howiya, it's Jackie. Can ye sort me out? Where are ye? Tallaght? Jaysus, hang on, I'm in a taxi, I'll hafte see if he'll bring me up."

Jackie turns to me beseechingly.

"Will ye drive is up te Tallaght? Please, I'm in bleedin' bits, I havte get sumtin in me before I go te work or I'll never las' de nigh? I'll sort ye out later on I swear."

She didn't look the best, and while I acknowledge that sticking another load of heroin in a vein wasn't necessarily the best way

31

forward, I wasn't going to throw her out of the car and leave her at the side of the road.

"Yeah right, but you better not mess me around," I said, half trying to imply that I'd sort her out if she didn't cough up later on.

"Ah, yer a star," she says, smiling and squeezing my knee before returning to Dave on the other end of my phone, "Dave? Yeah, dat's cool, he'll bring me up te ye. Whereabouts are ye? Oh, yer're goin' in te de pictures now, are ye? Well, leave yer fone on, yeah? Righ', talk te ye later, bye."

(Well at least that's one of life's mysteries unravelled. If, like me, you've often wondered what kind of moron leaves their phone on during a feature presentation, the answer is clear – customer service focused drug dealers.) Jackie hands me back my phone and smiles once more.

"Yer sound, d'ye know dat? Why're ye doin' 'dis anyway?" she asks.

"My good deed for the day I suppose," I say, shrugging my shoulders. "Where're you meeting this bloke?"

"He's in de pictures in de Square. I said I'd give 'im a call when we get dere."

I head for Tallaght and Jackie settles in, visibly more relaxed than she was five minutes ago. Then she turns to me and says, "I know you. I've met you before."

"Oh yeah?" I said, wondering whether I might have dropped her down to the bridge before or brought her home early one morning after work.

"Yeah, I never forget a face. Wassen in a car dough, tink it was a party somewhere."

"Wouldn't say so," I said, "I work nights all the time, don't really go to many parties." Which is true, as I find it too easy to say something I might not regret later on, and it justifiably kind of bugs both host and assembled guests.

"Well it wassen in a pub, 'cos I don't really drink a lot, an' I'm nearly sure it wassen in a car. Ye weren't down fer business yerself one nigh' were ye?" she says matter-of-factly.

Now, I'm no Casanova but I haven't yet resorted to paying for a shag. Not that the idea of it bothers me on a moral level at all, it's just business, each party knows what they're getting out of it, and the sooner our legislators follow the example set by our European neighbours in Holland and legalise it, the better for all concerned I reckon.

"No, not me, I might have dropped someone down to you before though. Where do you work from?"

"Waterloo Road," she said, "at de bus stop."

"Oh right, beside the lane up at the top, yeah?"

"Dat's it, yeah."

"Yeah, I probably dropped you down one night, or brought you home. Do you really remember every face, yeah?"

"Yeah, had a client de udder nigh' an' I new I new him from sumwhere, just cudden place it. Said 'is name was Martin, an' I …"

"Yeah, but was that his real name?" I interjected. "I mean, you're hardly gonna end up best friends. Why would someone tell you his real name?"

"Oh no, he was strayed up, he'd paid fer two hours, an' we were sittin' in de flat havin' a smoke. Anyway, I said I new 'is face an' den we started talkin' about people we new, and sure enough, hadden I med 'im at a weddin' down the country last year, so dere. Ye see, I never forged a face, dough it's more yer voice. Keep talkin', it'll come te me …"

I turned to have a good look at her. Despite what the contents of this book might suggest, I haven't had that many hookers in my car, and like Jackie, I too would like to think that I have a pretty good memory, and she did look vaguely familiar all right.

"I didn't get you one night I had this Yank in the car, did I? Going back to the Westbury, and then I collected you a couple of hours later and brought you back to the bridge?"

"Was dat when we had te go and get some coke in Dolphin? No, that was Peter's taxi. The Westbury?" she said, musing on it. "Jaysus, yeah, dat might be it, alldough I could 'ave sworn it wassen in a car, but it migh' 'ave bin, allrigh'."

"Jesus, that's mad isn't it? That was a couple of years ago. He was a total nutter that lad."

"Jus' playin' 'is little games, dat's all," she said, "no harm in it."

I suppose not, whatever floats your boat. At this stage we're up at Kilnamanagh, so I redial the last number on my phone and give it to Jackie, telling her to arrange a spot we can meet Dave at. Obviously unperturbed at the annoyance and discomfort he was causing to his fellow cinema goers in the UCI, Dave promptly answers his phone and suggests the taxi rank outside as the rendezvous. I park at the back of the rank and Jackie gets out, returning less than a minute later, happy as a kid who got exactly what she wanted at Christmas.

"Deadly," she says, somewhat ironically I mused to myself, "dat's me sorted fer de nigh'. Listen, tanks a million fer doin' dis, I'm in bits. Now, we'll just go back te de flat, and I'll get dis in me, and den ye can drop me down te work, and I'll meet ye later on an' sort ye out wit what I owe ye."

"Yeah, fair enough," I said, as I headed out of the complex and back towards Harold's Cross.

"Dave's sound, ye know? Never let ye down. See dat, de way he came out of the pictures fer me? Not many'd do dat," she said, rather naïvely I thought. Surely it was in Dave's best interest to sort her out. He wasn't doing it for nothing, and as any marketing consultant will tell you, it's easier to retain an existing customer than it is to win a new customer.

Jackie was staring at her bag of heroin, rolling it between two fingers, though bag was too generous a word for it. It was tiny, about the size of a kernel, something like that.

"€80 for that, one in the mornin' an' one in the evenin', €160 a day I spend on this shit," she muses out loud.

"How long are you buying from him?" I ask her.

"'Bout two monts now."

Nearly ten grand in two months, unbelievable.

"Do you ever think about all the shit you could buy with that money if you weren't using?"

"Yeah, I know, it's a lot innit? I mean, I know I'll die if I don't stop usin', but it's hard te get help."

"What about Coolmine or somewhere like that?"

"Jaysus, I'd go in dere in the mornin' but dere's a waitin' list de lent of yer bleedin' arm."

As I go through the KCR, Jackie asks me to turn up the radio. There's a Guns 'n' Roses tune playing, "Cold November Rain". I oblige and Jackie starts singing faintly along. As the song fades out, she tells me of a taxi driver she knew a while back. He had picked her up a couple of times and they got to know each other. He used to take her to Spar in Rathmines for a coffee or a bite to eat during the night. It got to the stage where he used to pay her dealer for her gear so she wouldn't have to stand at a bus stop on Waterloo Road. They never got involved romantically she said, just friends. She didn't question his motives. I suppose when you're a hooker and an addict, you're not going to be moving in circles that would be conducive to the making of new friends, so you'd take friendship wherever you found it.

Turned out one night Jackie and this taxi driver were up in the Phoenix Park, sitting in his car. She was trying to find a vein to shoot up and he was just sitting there watching her. She couldn't get a hit, and after a few minutes he broke down crying. Told her about his girlfriend who had died from an overdose about ten years previously. He knew she was an addict and he was trying to help her sort herself out. One night he came home from work and she was slumped on the floor in the bathroom. He picked her up to carry her out to the car, but she died in his arms in the hall. He never got involved with anyone else afterwards, just drove his taxi and went home. Jackie was heading over to England to have an abortion, and he was trying to convince her to come home straight away afterwards, and that he'd keep an eye on her. Apparently, he used to love Guns 'n' Roses and before she went away he made her a copy of the tape and wrapped it up all pretty for her and gave it to her as a present. Jackie said she ended up staying in England for about four months after the abortion and used to play the tape over and over.

Heavy shit, this girl has been through it all, and still managed to remain reasonably upbeat about both life in general and the realities of the life she was leading. I pull up at the park in Harold's Cross where I had first met her and stop the car.

"Righ'," she says firmly, "I'll owney be a minit. Ye'll wait here fer me, won't ye?" she asks, squeezing my arm tightly.

"Yeah, sure, off you go," I said, bemused at my seemingly encouraging tone, knowing what she was going off to do.

Out she gets and across the road she goes. I have to admit I was curious to see the difference in her once she had injected herself. I've never done heroin and don't intend to at any time in the near future, but I am kind of voyeuristic about life in general, and have always heard that there's nothing quite like the rush of heroin. I had just spent the last forty minutes with Jackie and now she was going into her flat to shoot up, and I wanted to see the effect it had on her. The light goes on in her flat and I light up a smoke. Meter is reading about twenty-two euros at this stage, but I'm not that concerned about the money really. A punter knocks on the window and gestures towards town. I shake my head regretfully and he walks off, giving me the finger as he goes. After a couple of minutes, the light in Jackie's flat goes off and the front door opens. Eighty euros gone in six minutes. She skips lightly down the steps and straight out on to the road. Cars blow their horns as she dances backwards and forwards between lanes. I don't know how she didn't get knocked down and killed. She gets in the car and smiles.

"Oh yeah, I feel a lot bedder now. Have ye got a cigarette?" she asks slowly.

I give her a smoke and light her up before heading for Waterloo Road.

"Righ', what time is it?" she asks me.

"Eleven-forty," I say.

"Oh, I'm nod in de yewmur fer dis ad all," she says, slumping back in her seat, "really don't want te work tonigh' at all, but I hafte get money fer Dave – I owe him fer yesterdey as well – hafte get money fer you, and I wanna buy a new telly as well, so it has te be dun."

As I near Waterloo Road, Jackie suggests one last smoke before we part company. I'm not looking forward to the rest of the night either, though it couldn't begin to compare in unpleasantness to what lay ahead of her, and agree. I cruise around a bit and eventually park up, ironically, in front of the Albany Women's Clinic on Lower Fitzwilliam Street. A squad car passes by and slows down to have a look as I turn off my lights.

"Dey'll be back around now in a minit. Dey know me face well. Got cautioned last week an' all," Jackie says, taking a cigarette and lighting up.

"How long are you using?" I ask her bluntly.

"Owney tree years now," she says.

"And how old are you?"

"Thirty-four."

"You married?"

"Not any more. Got married when I was nineteen. Me da was a bid of an alcoholic, used te knock is around when 'e was locked. Me ma died den, an' we all left de gaf as soon as we cud. First fella dat ast me te marry 'im, I said yeah."

"And did he look after you?"

"Fer a while yeah, he wuz alrigh'. Den he got real possessive, cudden do antin on me own, go out wit me mates or antin. Had five kids wid 'im an' all."

"Five?" I ask incredulously. "Do you see them at all?"

"Once a week, if I'm lucky. Eldest lad is fifteen, he's great 'e is," Jackie says, her voice trembling a little as I dig a bit deeper.

Time to go really. This isn't O'Gorman's people and I'm not in any position to be giving people life counselling. I put out my cigarette, start the car and swing around to head back towards Jackie's bus stop.

I drop her off and give her my mobile number so she can call me to arrange to meet and sort out her taxi tab, and we say goodbye. I cruise off and do a bit. There's a few out at this stage and I'm kept going for a while.

Later on I'm out in Blackrock dropping some darlings up to Club 92 when the phone rings. It's about one thirty at this stage, and sure enough it's Jackie, wanting to meet up to settle her account. I suggest that I can be in Harold's Cross in about twenty minutes, but that's no good, she's on a roll and wants to go back out straight away. She promises to ring back later, says she'll be working until about five, as I will be to make up for those bastards towing my car earlier on.

As it happened, I got into a good groove and was kept going

until about six in the morning. No word from Jackie, so I headed for the Maxol in Harold's Cross to fill up before I went home, which is actually where I was going in the first place before my competitive streak got the better of me and I first came into contact with Jackie.

Thought I might hear from her the following night, but I didn't. Actually had two lads from Armagh down for the match who were looking for some entertainment and thought I'd throw some business her way, but she wasn't at her bus stop when I went by, so I didn't get my thirty euros and the lads didn't get laid.

Have bike, will deal

Tuesday, the 23rd of July, 2002, 10.30pm. (The date and time aren't really of any major significance, I suppose, just a reflection on my improved recording of events. You see some of these stories were written as sample chapters and dispatched to eight publishers to whet their appetites. Two of them said no thanks, four never replied and two were interested, with the good folk at Gill & Macmillan having the cop to snap me up quickly. So now that I have scored a publishing deal, I am happy to be more diligent in the notation of the details of various encounters.)

Anyway, touring around looking for a fare. I cruise down the North Circular past Phil Ryan's and through the lights at Ballybough where this one flags me down outside the Sunset Lounge on Portland Row. She used the old drunkenly-slapping-an-eight-year-old-on-the-head technique which you may recall really annoys me, but it being a quiet Tuesday during the "summer" with no students out, I gladly pull in. She looked a bit the worse for wear from a distance, and these initial observations were confirmed as soon as she opened the door.

"Alright cock, just gowing down the road an' back up."

Cockney bird. She gestures frantically at her friend across the road to hurry up and then clambers in the back, lethargically turning around to pull her bag after her like it was a sack of potatoes. Her friend, a small plump woman with peroxide blonde hair, totters across the road and hops in, pausing briefly to suck half a cigarette into her lungs before flicking the butt across the bonnet of my car.

"I haven got time fer dis, I really fuckin' don't," she says, slamming the door shut.

"Oh relax will you, we'll only be a minute," the cockney bird replies, before giving me her full attention. She props herself between the front seats and it was then I noticed how dilated her pupils were, eyes bursting out of her head.

"We gotta go down to Sheriff Street an' ven back up 'ere, alright mate?" she said.

"Yeah, fine," I replied, now getting a clearer idea of what they were up to. Didn't really bother me, I have to say. Live and let live. If you get hooked on that shit and screw up your life, tough. If you get hooked and sort yourself out, fair play. So I tip off down the road towards Seville Place and the Eastender fills blondie in with the details.

"Nah, you see wot happened right, wot happened was, that this geezer outta my job yeah, he said he'd sort me out wiv some mets yeah, and then he never came frew wiv it, so now I gotta go down here and just get somefing to last me a couple o' days yeah?"

"An' who's dis we're going te?"

"I got 'is numbe offis geezer at work, said he'd sort me out, yeah? Now, I'll jus' get me money ready ..."

Your one starts rooting through her bag and produces a seriously crumpled fifty-euro note. Blondie takes it off her and pushes it in my direction.

"Don't give 'im dat, ye won't see any bleedin' change. Here mister, can ye change dat fer is?"

We're stopped at the lights at the junction of Amiens Street, so I take the fifty and give her two twenties and a ten to make her deal. I check the note quickly to make sure it's real. Feels okay, but I make a note to pass it off in Spar later on just in case. Don't want to get sussed at the credit union with dodgy notes.

"Tanks very much. Now, here, jus' give 'im dat, righ? Now, put de rest away in yer bag, and leave it in de car. Where ye meetin' 'im?"

Blondie knows the drill alright, could have written a chapter in the Rough Guide for visiting junkies.

"I 'ave 'is number in me fone, said to meet 'im at the church. I'll give 'im a ring now."

The lights change and I head down Seville Place. The cars in front of me stop suddenly under the bridge and I hit the brakes. A forty-foot behind me heading for the port blows his horn so I respond with a blast of mine. Hold up is nothing to do with me. Some tourist in a 02 Micra rental is executing a nine-point turn in the middle of the bloody road. Either lost or decided that this particular part of Dublin wasn't quite what they were looking for on their holidays, and who could blame them. Blondie freaks at all the racket and starts screaming at me.

"Jaysus, turn left here mister, quick will ye? Turn bleedin' left!"

"What's up with you?" I snap back at her. "You said you wanted Sheriff Street, yeah?"

"I know yeah, we do, it's jus' dat bleedin' lurry has me freaked, jus' get outta his way will ye?"

I let out one of my speciality sighs and oblige, pulling into the side of the road so the asshole in his forty-foot penis extension can get by. Blondie recovers her composure and we proceed.

"Now, turn righ' here, no sorry de nex' one, at de railins, yeah?"

I make the turn on to Sheriff Street as junkie is online with the dealer, giving her ETA and establishing a rendezvous.

"… yeah right mate, nah we're jus' coming up to it now, yeah? Where are you? On a bike, yeah? Oh right, I see you now, 'ang on a minit."

She pops her head in my direction to bring me up to speed.

"Can you 'ang on 'ere a minit mate? Jus' going to sorf somefing out, yeah? Just 'ere by the end of the railings."

"You better hurry up, I'm not hanging around here all night," I reply. Last thing I needed was to get busted by the law for assorting with this lot. I pull in and she hops out. Very sprightly when she wants to be. The dealer casually cycles down the cobblestones on his no-doubt-stolen-from-Trinity-that-afternoon mountain bike. Must have been all of fifteen. Wearing standard issue counterfeit brand name tracksuit and baseball cap. Should have been out doing bob-a-job at his age but was obviously more content serving his time in the infinitely more lucrative narcotics industry. He stalls a few yards from the car and gives me the once over, deftly flips off his baseball cap and removes a little packet from the customised seam. Blondie advises me to get my turn in now so we can be ready for the off, but I ignore her. The other one grabs the packet and gives him a twenty. He stuffs the money into his pocket and nods curtly at her, turns his bike around and cycles back up to his mates who are whiling away the summer on a nearby wall.

Your one gets back into the car, visibly relieved at having got sorted out. Blondie takes the packet from her and verifies the authenticity of the stash.

"Yeah, dat's the biz alrigh', now let's go."

"Nice one, 'e's sound, said to give 'im a call if I needed anyfing else."

I reverse back down to the main road and swing around without saying a word. I head back towards Portland Row and then the cockney bird makes a request.

"'Scuse me mate, what's your name?"

"Alan," I reply.

No it's not, you're saying, checking the cover again. You're right, it's not, but Alan is my stage name if you like. If there's a seriously cute girl in transit and we're having a laugh I might divulge my real name if it is actively solicited, but by and large I have absolutely no desire to become intimately involved with the vast majority of punters in my car, and consequently refer to myself as Alan in such situations.

"Right Alan, I was wonnering if you could do me a favour."

Didn't like the sound of this and immediately started preparing my excuse. She reaches into her bag and pulls out a foot pump which she thrusts in my direction.

"You see this right? Could you help me pump up the tyres on my jeep? I 'ad a row wiv my boyfriend vis morning and he's gone an' let the air out of my tyres, yeah? So I 'ad to borrow vis to pump vem up yeah?"

Just going through the lights at the Five Lamps and a squad car cruises down in the opposite direction. Timing is everything, isn't it? Two minutes earlier and the boys would have got an easy bust and I would have got a whole load of grief trying to explain my innocence.

"Jaysus, it's yer own bleedin' fault he dun it!" blondie says. "Ye shagged his best mate!"

Sharon reflects on this a moment, and then nods her head.

"Yeah, I know vat ... but, still an' all, it were a long time ago wunnit?" she says, "anyway, fack 'im an' his moods, I jus' wanna get me tyres pumped up, go 'ome an' get out ovit, yeah? So, Alan, can you givus an' 'and or what?"

Blondie intervenes again and comes to my rescue.

"No he bleedin' can't, he has te earn a livin' an' I have te get back te the little uns before me ma gets home or she'll freak."

My thoughts exactly. Blondie's delinquent kids were home alone and my much-needed forthcoming holiday in Biarritz to escape precisely these situations was coming up soon and required some serious spending money.

"Sorry, no can do, I have a job to do in a few minutes. I'll drop you off here, alright?" I said, as politely as I could.

"Oh, alright ven, fanks anyway, yeah?" she says, gathering her stuff together. She turns to blondie to say goodbye.

"Tah-rah ven, I'll call over to the 'ouse some night, yeah?"

"No, I'll give ye a call soon, I'm stayin' in me ma's gaf, me house got burned, I'm waitin' on anudder one," blondie explained casually, as though the destruction by fire of one's abode were an everyday occurrence. I smiled to myself whilst envisaging what kind of crazy sequence of events led to her house being burnt down. Your one takes in the information as though these things happen all the time – which they probably do to certain people I supposed, but most of them live in Belfast don't they? – and nods her head in agreement.

"Alright ven, night night."

She gets out and a by now exasperated blondie pulls the door closed after her.

"Jaysus tonigh', ye'd never be done wit her, d'ye know dat? I'm jus' goin' around de korner te de flats mister, righ? Me little fella'll be goin' spare."

I swing around the corner and head along Summerhill Parade, pulling in at the flats as requested, skilfully manoeuvring between the stolen bikes, discarded clothing and rusting prams that lay strewn along the road like an obstacle course in a poor man's Krypton Factor grand final.

"Now, that's €6.80 please," I said, totalling the meter. It was actually €6.85, but I never bother with the five cents on a fare, it's too much grief.

"Now, dere's seven sumtin dere, bid o' shrapnel fer ye, alrigh'?" she says, handing me a load of coins.

"Yeah that's cool, thanks a lot, good luck," I reply.

She clambers over the seat to the far door and gets out, slams the door and trots over to the stairwell, shouting up to someone on one of the balconies as she goes. One junk run a night is enough for me so I switch my roof light off and head towards the somewhat more predictable environs of the rank at the Burlo.

The Runner

've had a few runners in my time, not that many though, maybe six or seven over the course of the last few years, which isn't too bad I suppose. Had a few lads who no doubt planned to do a runner whilst hailing a taxi, but then changed their minds when they saw me, figuring that I might chase after them because, unlike a lot of taxi drivers, I wasn't fat and fifty and I didn't like taking shit from anyone. Those lads would have got away with it and all though, because, quite apart from the fact that the repercussions of me running a hundred yards would take up a whole episode of ER, I just couldn't be arsed running after some toe rag for the sake of a tenner.

Normally you can actually feel a runner situation evolve as the journey progresses. I had one shortly after I started taxi driving where two lads in the car told me they had to call into a mate's house in Firhouse on the way home, allegedly to collect a Playstation game. We get to the house in question and the lad in front gets out, goes up the driveway and pretends to ring the bell. The lad in the back starts acting all impatient and says he'll go and see what the delay is. When I heard this, I sussed what they were up to and lunged towards the back seat to grab him but the little shit got out. The first lad sees his accomplice has made his exit and the two of them hare towards a wall at the end of the cul-de-sac we were in and bound over it. I hopped out and gave pursuit, but the vast expanse of fields on the far side of the wall convinced me of the futility of the exercise, and I returned to my idling car, a tenner the poorer.

Now I have a big Volvo with remote locking so if a break for freedom is attempted, I can hit the button and stall the intended exit of the toe rag in question. Another handy thing about the Volvo is that the door release mechanism is a lever rather than a conventional pull-handle and is actually somewhat secreted in the door panel itself, so intending absconders not familiar with the interior layout of the Swedish marque might find the speed of their egress somewhat impeded.

But on this particular night, the chap in question didn't make a run for it as such, so the previously lauded design feature didn't come into play. He simply vanished into thin air.

It was the night of Ireland's paradoxically glorious and ignominious exit from the 2002 World Cup and the streets were hopping. I had started earlier than usual, straight after the match, and had been going at it full tilt all night. By this stage it was about 3am and I was looking to head home to Bray, so I cruised up to Leeson Street looking for some Dalkey darlings to bring home. However, as soon as I turned the corner from Pembroke Street, I was stressed. Bloody taxis, horses and cops everywhere, people milling around the middle of the road like it was a pedestrianised plaza – it does my head in. I went straight through the lot of them and headed over the bridge around to the Burlo. Just past the rank a chap walking towards Donnybrook flagged me down, so I stopped, figuring he must be heading my way.

He hops in the front seat and starts up, all chat. Heading out to Foxrock – lovely – mad night, on the piss all day, drank himself sober with Fiachra and Oisín, etc., the usual south county Dublin shite. The last thing I needed at this hour of the morning was a talker, especially on the day that was in it – I'd had it up to my eyes with Joe Public's various theories on Keano, Mick, Dunphy *et al*, but I let him ramble on, throwing in a "Yeah" or a "You're dead right" every now and then.

I shoot up the dualler at a respectable eighty miles an hour, getting a lovely run through a series of amber lights and ask him if he wants a right up Brewery Road or at White's Cross. He kindly informs me that one or other of those bastard utilities contractors are "working" in Foxrock village and that there is no access on to Brighton Road from Torquay Road or Westminster Road so I should go on past the church at Kill Lane and turn right at Cornelscourt and go up the hill.

I tear up Cornelscourt Hill and as I finally turn right on to Brighton Road, he cuts short his delivery of a no doubt very informative treatise on the state of the Irish music industry and tells me to slow down as the entrance to his palatial family home is coming up. I turn as instructed onto a private road which serves as a common driveway for a number of substantial detached houses, each secluded on their own private grounds. I am then further directed to turn again into the appropriate house. I flick on my full beams as I cruise down the driveway to have a good look around and eventually arrive, some three hours later it seems, at the surface level car park serving his house, which bore an uncanny resemblance to a high-end used car dealership. A hundred grand executive beast for scion of industry daddy, a people carrier for mummy, and two trendy little runabouts for brat child number one and brat child number two.

Head the ball casually informs me that he has to go into the house to get some cash. I nod in agreement and he gets out and strolls around the corner of the house to the door. After a minute, I decide to get my turn in so as to be ready for the off and cruise around same corner to get a swing. I open my window and wait for the exchange of funds. And wait. And wait. After what seemed like an eternity, but was in fact probably more like five or six minutes, I start to get pissed off. I didn't suspect anything at this stage, I was just annoyed at having to wait so long for this asshole to arrive back with my money. There was a light on in the upstairs landing so I assumed he had gone in to get some money from his bedroom, which may have been located at the rear, in the south wing. All the same, it seemed kind of quiet though.

Another few minutes pass, and now I am seriously stressed. What is this moron at? I don't care how big a bloody house is, it couldn't take this long to get some cash and reappear. I get out of the car and go over to the living room window to have a look inside. Curtains are for appearances only in these kinds of houses, no need to draw them at night when the only person that can overlook your garden would have to be a qualified helicopter pilot. No sign of life there so I go over to the front door and have a look into the hallway. All quiet there too. Now, I still didn't think that he had done a runner on me. I figured he might have just slumped on to his bed and dozed off or something, though at this stage I secretly hoped that he had slipped in the bathroom and cracked his skull off one of the his 'n' hers sinks for messing me around.

After debating my options, I decided there was nothing for it but to ring the bell and wake the entire household and sort the situation out. Over the years I have developed a particular bell-ringing technique for precisely these types of situations. It basically consists of depressing the bell and holding it down until the door is answered.

(Heretofore, the record for a single ring was somewhere in the order of two minutes twenty seconds. I had been dispatched to collect somebody from a house on Leeson Street, and duly informed the base controller of my arrival. She rang the people concerned and they said they would be right out. They weren't. After a few minutes, I made the arduous trek up the granite steps and rang the bell politely. No answer. There was a light on in the tastefully decorated basement kitchen. I rang the bell again. Still no answer. So I rang it again, and this time let it ring and ring and ring, until some two minutes and twenty seconds later, the door was almost pulled off its hinges by this purple-faced asshole who started bellowing something along the lines of *If you ever do that again* .... I waited for him to finish and politely parried his pathetic threat with a confident declaration that he would never be brought anywhere in my taxi, then or at any time in the future. He immediately rang the taxi company and demanded I be summarily dismissed and my head brought to him on a silver platter, lightly garnished with a ring of fennel, a ridiculous demand they obviously did not accede to. Besides, where would you get fennel at that time on a Sunday night? Later, out of nothing but pure and wilful badness, I went back to his house when I was finishing up at around four in the morning. I left the engine running, got out of the car, hopped quietly up the granite steps and gave the bell a good long ring. I jumped back in the car and waited. Less than a minute later, the door was flung open by the same asshole, his white hair all tussled after being woken abruptly from fitful slumber. I beeped my horn, waved cheerfully and then tore off back to the base, breaking my shite laughing all the way. Ignorant and petty I hear you say. Possibly, but it's very therapeutic nonetheless. And that's how I developed my bell-ringing technique.)

So, I flex my index finger and ring the bell. It's obviously not used to being rung in such a sustained fashion and the volume dips and rises somewhat, but sure enough, after a minute or so, a bedroom light goes on and there is a mad scamper down the stairs. The door was answered by a woman in her fifties. (Botox isn't the answer ladies. Grow old gracefully.) Mummy was wearing tartan pyjamas – which didn't really do anything for her, or me for that matter – no slippers, no dressing gown.

"What is it? What's going on?" she screamed at me.

I would have thought that my seriously disgruntled demeanour and idling taxi three yards away might have been self-explanatory, but no, I was going to have to talk her through this one.

"Your son owes me twenty bloody euros for his taxi, that's what's going on. He went in to get the money over fifteen minutes ago and hasn't reappeared. Kindly locate him and get him out here."

She then switches on the exterior lights to make sure I wasn't the entry man for a gang of burglars who planned to ransack her home.

"*My* son? Owes *you* money for a taxi?"

Pleased that my basic command of the English language had managed to convey the nature of the situation to her, I nodded my head.

"Yes, that's correct. I brought him home from town and he said he was going inside to get money for the taxi. That was twenty minutes ago," I said, exaggerating the time elapsed so as to justify my frustration and seemingly dramatic actions.

The cool night air wakes her up somewhat and she gets herself together, nodding her head slowly.

"Right, okay, okay. I'll go and get him."

She closes the door and scampers back up the stairs. I return to the car to see what the meter is at. Nearly twenty-four bloody euros at this stage. I resolve to hold out for the full amount, inclusive of waiting time, and wait for asshole to emerge. A minute later, the door opens once again and mother pushes this lad in my direction. Not the same guy at all! What the fuck was this? The guy who got out of my taxi and ostensibly disappeared into this house was shortish with dark hair. This lad was about the same age, but tall and gangly, with already thinning hair and glasses, dressed in boxer shorts and white tee shirt. He approaches the car with a suitably bewildered look on his face, while mummy remains at the door, arms folded across her chest.

"What's the story man?" he says. "What's going on?"

I can't figure this one out at all, and after briefly explaining the sequence of events, suggest that maybe his mother woke up the wrong person and it's his brother I'm after.

"Look, I'm the only guy in this house, and I arrived home hours ago and paid for my bloody taxi," he says angrily.

"Fair enough, but all I know is that I brought a guy home from town to this house and he said he was going inside to get the money, and I haven't seen him since. I accept that you are not that person, but I am not hallucinating. Somebody got out of my taxi to go into this house and disappeared."

Your man looks around the forecourt and shrugs his shoulders.

"Yeah well, it wasn't me, man. I think you've been had. Whoever it was must have disappeared or something."

What powers of deduction! It was quite bloody obvious he disappeared. I just wanted to find him again and kick the living shit out of him before reversing over him repeatedly.

"Look, I told you what happened, alright? Are you not concerned about the fact that I drove some guy up to your front door and he disappeared into thin air?" I said, by now totally pissed off at the realisation of what had transpired.

"No, I'm not actually. I'm concerned about going back to bed if you must know."

A fair point really. Mother approaches the car to assess the situation.

"Excuse me," she says to me, "is this the person who was in your car?"

"No it's not," I conceded, "but I'm surprised that you don't seem too concerned at the thought of someone using your property as an escape route from my taxi."

"Well, if that's what happened, then that's what happened. It's got nothing to do with us whatsoever. Now, if you don't mind, I've had quite enough of this and would like to go back to bed. Is that alright?"

It wasn't alright as far as I was concerned, but what could I do? I apologised for the misunderstanding and mother and son retreated to the house and closed the door. I sat in the car for a minute wondering where the little bastard could have gone. I hopped out and had a quick look around to see where the possible escape route was. Couldn't make much out in the dark, so I got back in the car and drove slowly away, scanning the front garden as I went, hoping to see a figure lurking in the bushes. Nothing. I drove out and turned down the private road and into the next house, a surprisingly modest looking bungalow. No sign of life here either. I acknowledged that he was definitely gone and called off the manhunt.

I got back on to the main road and headed for Bray, musing aloud to myself at the sheer neck of the little shit. I resolved to commit his image to memory forever, and God help him if I ever see him again because he's going to end up stranded in the Sally Gap with severely impaired reproductive capabilities.

Romeo and Juliet

Now this one takes the biscuit. Out of about four years driving around this kip, this one really stands out.

The company I was renting the taxi from at the time had a lot of big accounts with hospitals, health boards, banks and solicitors. The hospitals were great, always on the phone, day and night. You could always get a few good jobs that could turn a crap night into an okay night. And so it was on this particular night. I got a handy job collecting bloods from the Meath – one up to the lab in James's and the other one out to Beaumont to the toxicology department. Coming back through Drumcondra the base controller gave me a shout and told me to head in to Temple Street to collect a nurse who was going over to Cherry Orchard to do a shift there. Farcical really, the state of the health service – a nurse clocks on for duty in one hospital and gets straight into a taxi to go and do that shift in another hospital across the city. And then gets a taxi back when she is finished. Not that I was complaining, because said chaotic shambles that is our national health service was earning me a few quid. So in I go, collect my passenger and shoot over to Ballyer.

I drop the nurse off at unit five. Sometimes it works out sweet and there's one there finishing a shift and you get to take her back, but not tonight so I head off back towards town. I'm driving down the road past the garage at the industrial estate and I see this lad stumbling along the path. He turns and sees me and starts waving his arm frantically. Looks a bit the worse for wear, but what's new? I pull over and he gets in the back.

"Alrigh' man, tanks fer stoppin'. I'm just goin' around de korner to me bird's gaf, but I can't walk, me fuckin' leg is killin' me!"

Now, as you know by now, I normally don't feel obliged to indulge punters in idle banter at all, but this chap seemed sound enough, and I hadn't said a word on my two previous trips, the first one being the bloods and I am not yet in the habit of speaking to inanimate objects, and the second one was the nurse out to Cherry Orchard itself. She was a narky cow, all snooty because I was late. I'm a taxi driver for God's sake, what did she expect? So I gave her the silent treatment all the way over. So now, maybe fearful of ending up like Robinson Crusoe and having to talk aloud to myself lest I forget how to, I converse.

"Oh yeah? What did you do to it?"

"I dun nuttin to it, it was me bird's aul fella, de bollix. He got me shot."

"You're kidding me! He got you shot?"

I pull over and turn around to have a look. Your man is half slumped across the back seat, resting on his elbow to take the weight off his leg. He nods his head and pulls up the leg of his jeans. A really poor dressing, obviously done by a mate or something, covered a wound on his shin. Blood was still coming through the bandage and was dripping down his leg. There was even blood on the mat on the floor, which didn't bother me in the slightest, because the piece of shit wasn't my car. Now this was a first, never had a shotgun victim in the car before, so I have to say I was intrigued.

"What the fuck did he do that for?"

"'Cos he's owney a prick, dat's why. Always badmouthin' me, tellin' her to drop me. Then las' week I was gargled and had id out wit him, told 'im to fuck off and leave is aloan. He flipped an' said he'd get me sorted out, yeah? He's always givin' it lodes, tinks he's rock hard. Said he'd get the RA to shoot me, so I says, 'Go on so, ye fat fuck'. An 'e bleedin' does!"

This was mad shit. Obviously just a warning shot, he wasn't dying or anything. If those boys wanted you out of the way permanently, I don't think they'd miss. But still, getting shot is getting shot.

"And what are you going over there now for?"

He looks at me as though I was the most stupid person he'd ever met.

"Gonna have it out wit the prick, dat's why! He told the RA I was sellin' drugs. Ye know what dey're like wit all dat shit, all vigilantes an' stuff. So bang in the fuckin' leg dis afternoon."

"And *are* you dealing?"

"No I'm bleedin' not man! Fuck's sake. I'm owney off de gear a few monts meself. I've a bleedin' kid wit her, I wooden do dat shit man, dey're owney scum."

I always go with my instincts when it comes to judging people, and I believed him straight away. I liked him too I have to say. I've a lot of time for people who get hooked on gear and come out the other side of it, and I've met a good few of them over the last number of years. Most people have no idea what that side of life is like, and ignorantly adopt a let-them-rot kind of mentality which is complete shit. This lad was about twenty-nine or so, same as myself at the time. You've no control over where you're born, or into what circumstances you're born, and life's a bitch at the best of times. So he fell off the straight and narrow, started using, but got himself clean again. He has a kid with this girl, who he's obviously mad about, and was just trying to sort his life out. And yet her father won't forget what he was like before and goes and gets him shot! I ask you!

"Will ye bring is over te de gaf?"

"Yeah sure, where is it?"

"Cherry Orchard. I'll show ye, hang a righ' here bud."

So off we go. I hang a right and then a right again, over all the poxy ramps. It's true what they say; you do get an infinitely better quality of ramp in Blackrock than you do in Ballyfermot, regardless of the higher incidence of joyriding in the latter. Down to the end of the road and around a little roundabout and into the badlands. It was then anyway, I know it's been cleaned up a lot in the last few years, houses fixed up properly and all that, but back then it was dodge city.

"Which one is it?"

Your man was still propping himself up, nodding his head as if helping to propel me further down the road.

"Yeh, dis is it here. Alrigh, you stall it here an' I'll go in. Will ye hang on fer us? I won't be able te walk back, d'ye know whad I mean?"

Now, two things to point out here. First, you're dead right *I'll* stall it here and *you'll* go in. And second, of course I'm going to hang on. There's no way I'm missing this shit. Only wish I had a camcorder with me.

"Yeah, yeah, 'course I will man, don't worry. Take it easy, alright?"

He sits up and opens the door, turning himself around in the seat the way old people have to, to make his exit as painless as possible, cursing the perpetrator of his misfortune as he does so. He walks, or rather hobbles, along the path and angrily kicks open the stubborn gate to the house, shouting as he goes.

"Karina! Karina! Come out an' see wha he's after doin' te me! Karina!"

Before Karina can do anything, the door swings open and this big, fat, mean, burly bastard strides out. The father, I'm guessing. He marches down the drive and starts pushing your man, trying to shove him out of the driveway. My man wasn't for turning though.

"Fuck off yew, ye bollix! It's yew dat has me like this ye prick! Couden sort sumtin' out yerself. Ye have te go tellin' lies about me te de RA, so dey'd do it!"

"Shut yer face, ye junkie scum! Nex time, dey'll sort ye out fer good, I'm warnin' ye! Now fuck off!"

Then a window upstairs opens and a girl, obviously Karina, sticks her head out. She was in a right state, obviously been crying her eyes out.

"Bosco! Leave it will ye? Jus leave it, I'll talk te ye temorrow, righ'?"

The father is aghast at this treachery and shouts up at her.

"No ye fuckin' won't, righ'? We've bin over dis an' dat's dat. Now close dat bleedin' winde!"

"Karina, come down here, I jus want te talk te ye Karina. He's owney a bollix, spreadin' shite about me. You know I'm not dealin'. I wooden do dat, ye know I wooden!"

"I know yer not Bosco, alrigh? Now jus leave it will ye? I'll see ye temor …!"

Again, pops interjects to disagree, and points his finger up at the window.

"No ye fuckin' won't see him temorrow! Or de day after," and then turning around to resume shoving Bosco, "and yew, fuck off, I'm warnin' ye, righ'?"

(On a classical note, I was struck by the resemblance of this scene to one penned by the bard in his seminal work *Romeo and Juliet*. You know, boy loves girl, father of girl doesn't approve, etc., etc. I think it was the upstairs window that did it, which is probably the closest thing you'll get to a balcony in Ballyfermot.)

Then the mother comes out in to the driveway. She had been standing at the hall door for a few minutes and must have felt a woman's touch was now needed.

"Lookit, yew jus go home te yer ma, and give it a rest, will ye? And yew, get back inside the house, yer makin' a fuckin' show o' yerself!"

At this point, I was waiting for Roddy Doyle to emerge and say "Cut!", while some production runners got coffee for the cast as make up and hair were attended to and lighting adjusted, but no, this was the real deal. Barrytown supplanted to Ballyfermot.

My man Bosco was obviously feeling a bit weak with all the exertion and had moved over to lean on the dividing wall to support himself. He wasn't through though, and addresses the mother.

"Lookit, ye know I'm not dealin' bleedin' drugs! We've gotta kid fer fuck's sake. Tell him te back off and leave is a-bleedin-loan!"

"I don't know what yer doin' or not doin', but she's not comin' out te ye, alrigh? Now go home te yer ma an' we'll sort dis out layder."

"No, I want te sort it out now. Look wha' he's after doin' te me! Me fuckin' leg is in tatters 'cos o' him! I jus want te speak te Karina fer a second, it's not fuckin' fair!"

The neighbours had heard the commotion at this stage and were out in force on their doorsteps smoking cigarettes or sitting on walls discussing the merits and demerits of each party's argument. The father had turned to go back in and addressed them.

"Whad are youse bleedin' lookin' at? Fuck off back inside yis nosy bastards!"

Now, in my book, nosy would be putting a glass against a wall to try and eavesdrop. This was on a different scale altogether, this was aggro in public, and as such, the neighbours were, I felt, as I was, entitled to look on and draw their own conclusions. The father gives Bosco a final "I'm fuckin' warnin' ye!" and goes inside. For a second I thought he maybe had a gun in the house and was going to sort this out there and then, but he just slams the door. The light in the upstairs window goes off, and a second later, the door opens again. It's Karina, in flagrant breach of paternal instructions. The mother runs towards her, trying to prevent her from coming any further, but is repelled.

"Karina, go back inside, now isn't de time fer dis."

A logical point I felt, but Karina took no heed.

"Stoppit ma. Yew go in an' keep him quiet, I'll owncy be a minit. Go on!"

The mother relents and opens the door to go in, pausing for a second to look back at the situation. She shakes her head ruefully and closes the door. Karina walks over to Bosco and sits on the wall beside him, putting her arm around his shoulder. He is close to tears now, the poor bastard. The neighbours, disappointed that nothing out of the ordinary has happened, shuffle back indoors, leaving the troubled couple alone on the wall to have a talk, which they do, with lowered voices so I can't really hear what's going on.

After a few minutes, the front door opens again and the father reappears. Round two I thought, but he just stands there. Bosco starts to stand, but Karina diplomatically guides him towards the gate and my waiting taxi, hushing him as she does so. She opens the door of the car and helps him in.

"Go home Bosco. I'll see ye tomorrow."

Bosco sniffles and nods his head in agreement.

"Yeah righ, I'll see ye den love. An' don't be listenin' te dat prick, ye know whad he's like ..."

"Shush Bosco, don't start or ye'll have 'im on yer case again. Bye."

She cups his face in her hands and gives him a kiss on the cheek. He smiles at her and nods his head.

"G'nigh'. I luv ye."

Seriously tender shit. Nearly had me going and as a rule I don't encourage public displays of affection at all. The door closes and I turn around.

"Alright? You going home now yeah?"

"Yeah bud, tanks fer waitin', ye're a star. Back out te de main road an' I'll show ye."

Back over the ramps and across the road into one of the other estates. I pull up outside the house and Bosco reaches into his pocket to get some cash.

"I've only got a fiver on me bud, but I can go inte de gaf an' get de rest. How much is it?"

The meter was ticking all through the drama, but I wasn't worried. I like seeing this side of life, really wakes you up to stuff. I took the fiver alright, but I left it at that.

"You're alright man, don't worry about it."

"Ye sure? I can ged it off de aul dear like. She's probly in bed, bud I can wake her."

"No, no, it's cool, don't worry about it."

"Sound, tanks man. Tanks a lot, an' tanks fer waitin fer me."

"No problem, hope everything works out."

"Bang on bud. Cheers."

Bosco opens the door and gets out slowly, resting his hand on the car as he makes his way towards his house. He opens the door quietly so as not to wake his sleeping mother and goes in, pausing at the door for a second to give me a quick wave.

"Lucan, please"

Cruising down Merrion Row, Thursday evening, about ten o'clock. January, and the streets are dead. Everybody's broke after the Christmas, shitting the arrival of their Visa bills like they were the Leaving results, or hanging on to a few quid to book the summer holiday. Either way, they weren't out on a Thursday, official start of the weekend or not, pissing it away in the pub like they're supposed to, inconsiderate bastards.

The base controller calls for a car on the green. Trigger finger does the business and I get the job – Holles Street for cash. Don't like hospital jobs much – you never know what you're going to be landed with – junkies, winos, scumbags, hookers, you name it. Holles Street wasn't so bad though, being a maternity hospital. Normally "good" news, if that's what you're into. (Which I'm not.)

So. Down Merrion Square, hang a right, narrowly avoiding one of those Aircoach buses, the driver of which was taking the "express service" element of their product offering a little too seriously by careering through the red lights. What an asshole. Has no one told him that flagrantly breaking red lights, as well as never indicating, is a privilege afforded only to taxi drivers?

Park outside the hospital on the double yellow line. Switch on hazard lights, thereby rendering car invisible, hop out and kick door closed behind me. I go into the lobby and raise my eyebrows expectantly at porter, who points in the direction of my passenger. Female, late twenties, slim, dark hair, cute in a kind of wholesome way. Give her the eyebrow treatment and gesture towards the car. She nods her head slowly and gets up to follow me. In we get and off we go.

"Where're you off to?"

"Lucan, please."

"No problem."

Which it isn't, but it's a pain in the arse. Lucan. Hate the place. Eight hundred and seventy nine little "Surrey-style" cul-de-sacs of poor quality, over-priced new homes, thrown up in a few weeks by developers who couldn't give a shit if they fell down in a month. The Avenue. The Close. The Court. The Crescent. The Downs. The Drive. The Glen. The Grove. The Rise. The Walk. The Way. You get the idea. The one that really gets me is The Green, which basically means there was a troublesome 200-year-old oak tree in the middle of a field that the developers weren't allowed knock down, and so, on the advice of their resourceful architects, they turned it into a "design feature" and spared both tree and a few thousand blades of grass from an otherwise certain death. Then, those savvy marketing kids hit upon the novel idea of using the now majestic, not troublesome, tree as the visual cornerstone of their promotional literature, in a thinly veiled attempt to give the development an air of maturity, lulling prospective buyers to this idyllic haven, where they and their families could live and grow as a community in the bosom of mother nature.

However, my dislike of Lucan does not stem entirely from

cute hoor developers flogging unimaginatively designed houses. No, the big thing about Lucan with me is the roundabouts. Every time I go out there a new one has materialised to serve as the access and egress for yet another new exclusive estate. (Sorry, "development". Apologies to Gunne, Leahy Estates, Sherry Fitzgerald *et al.* As if you and I didn't know that "exclusive" is estate agent speak for the fact that phase one – of eleven – has "only" ninety-three "units".) So God help you when you're trying to get back out of the place, especially when it's dark. A wrong exit off one of the roundabouts, and that's it, you're lost in a maze of estates filled with architecture-by-numbers houses that all look the bloody same. There's nothing for it but to launch the distress flare, check the glove box for emergency food supplies, and hope that the ensuing Air Corps rescue won't take too long.

Anyway, Lucan. Pearse Street, the quays, and on out along the dualler. No chit chat as yet, which isn't at all unusual in my taxi. In fact it's the norm. I never feel obliged to talk to punters. It's an A to B transaction; good times are extra as the man says, whoever he is. I know whenever I'm in the back seat myself I'm hoping against hope that the gobshite doesn't start boring me to death with his pathetic slant on life, much as I am doing now, to you my complicit reader. Sometimes an uneasy atmosphere develops, particularly on a long journey like this one. Never bothers me though. I actually quite enjoy the way it makes people feel uncomfortable, asshole that I am.

But this time it was different. I'm naturally perceptive – as one who meets about two hundred people every week ought to be – and as soon as she got into the car I knew something was amiss. Leaving a maternity hospital on her own, sad not happy. Miscarriage, possibly. As we pass through Palmerstown I hear a soft sobbing in the back of the car. Checking the rearview mirror, I see she has her head in her hands. Shit, that's rough. And no boyfriend, husband, mother or sister there to give her a hug and say something stupid but nice like "it'll be alright", or "it wasn't meant to be", or "you've plenty of time, you can try again". Just me, and the whole kids thing is not my forte, believe me. Don't have any, don't want any. Take up too much time, limit your options, cost you a fortune, piss you off, wreck your head, break your heart, etc. etc.

But that wasn't the way she saw it, obviously. Her little baby had died before it was even born. And there was nothing she could do about it, except get a taxi home on her own to Lucan. And if that wasn't bad enough, her misfortune is compounded by having said taxi driven by an asshole like me, who couldn't for one minute get past his own cynical and self-absorbed assessment of the way things are and the way they should be, and say something nice like "it'll be all right".

Up the flyover at The Foxhunter and left. Down to the first roundabout and straight through, I reckoned. Have to ask her for directions soon, and the sobbing is getting louder, more frequent.

"Sorry, straight on, is it?"

"Em, sorry, where are we?" She wipes her eyes and straightens herself up, looking out the window to get her bearings.

"Left at this roundabout, straight through the next one, and then left into the estate please."

"Right so."

On we go another little bit, and then into the estate.

"Whereabouts are you?"

"Sorry," she says, coughing, trying to get it together. "Next left, right and second on the right."

"Right so."

Make mental note for the way out – left, second left, right and right out the gates.

"Just here's fine, thanks. How much is that?"

Still haven't brought myself to say anything that would let her know that I do actually give a shit about her loss and hope that everything works out for her. I hope she has a significant other on his way home to her. Or if he is away on business or whatever, that he remembers to call home to see how she is and say goodnight, and let her cry down the phone to him about what happened.

We do the money thing, I say thanks and take care, and I mean it. She manages to crack the faintest smile, gets out and walks slowly around the corner into the cul-de-sac.

Wayne, Texas Ranger

Quiet enough Wednesday night. Really wasn't in the mood for working at all. I usually start around seven, when all the nine-to-five wage slaves have finally made it home to the burbs and here it was, only eight o'clock and I was pissed off already. Decided to go up to the rank at the Westbury and sit it out for a while. And yes, it is a rank. For taxis *only*. It is not, as most residents of south county Dublin seem to think, a really handy place to park whilst you run around Grafton Street indulging in a bit of retail therapy. I pull up outside the hotel, making sure to park in such a way that there is not enough room either in front of me or behind me for some tosser to park a car.

So there I am, seat reclined, reading *The Phoenix*. Great job your man has. I'd love it. Exposing all the skulduggery that passes for standard business tactics today. The only downer would be the whole people-in-glass-houses bit. You couldn't put a foot wrong yourself or all the bastards you'd hung out to dry in the past would have you for breakfast. Still, it'd be cool all the same. Anybody that pissed you off, bang out a few hundred words slagging them off for not filing returns or for knocking up unauthorised developments. Shit, the amount of people I know that I don't like, I'd have to change the publishing format from fortnightly to daily.

My reading was interrupted by a knock on the window. The hotel porter enquired as to whether or not I was free for a couple of hours. Oh, I liked the sound of this. Could be a country run, set me up nicely for the weekend. I nodded affirmatively and readied myself for action. The porter opens the front passenger door and turns to my intended occupant, a big fat fellow who was standing under the canopy. Obviously an American. Not just because he was clinically obese, even though that's normally a safe enough starting point, but because he was wearing cowboy boots, *ironed* jeans, checked shirt, sports jacket with leather elbow patches, cowboy hat and one of those stupid S&M-looking leather accessories in place of a tie, with an eagle hanging off the end of it. I kid you not. I was half expecting him to ask me to take him to some shitty ballroom of romance in Clare where he was competing in the final of some international hillbilly tobacco-chewing line dancing competition. He probably would have scored highly on presentation, but poorly on technical merit on account of the fact that his considerable girth would have prevented him from properly executing the more complex moves.

Anyway, in he gets and tips the hat at me. Now he's just taking the piss, I thought, but then he starts talking and this guy was the genuine article – a real live American wacko.

"Good evenin' sir, how you doin'? Mah name's Wayne Jackson, and I'm a private investagator from the Yew-nited States. I was wonerin' if you might be available for hire for a couple hours to assist me in mah work?"

This was a new one on me, so I was playing along. (Banged the meter on straight away of course. Wacko or no wacko, he wasn't getting a free ride from me.)

"Yeah, sure thing. What's up?" I said.

Wayne reaches inside his jacket and produces a piece of paper. He unfolds it and hands it to me to examine as he explains his quest.

"Thing is friend, I have been retained by a prominent Irish-American family from the ease coas to track down their missin' dawder. Family were on vay-cation in Kerry, arrived aboud a week ago. Everythang seemed to be jus' fine, and then she upped and left a couple days ago."

So far, so weird. I looked at Wayne, half expecting him to swear me in as a temporary agent the way the FBI do to kids in movies when they know the whereabouts of some nutter the feds want to shoot on sight. But alas, no silver star for me. Wayne continued in earnest.

"The parents of this young lady are naturally very concerned 'bout her well being an' believe she may have come to Dublin. She spent some time here last summar and may have hooked up with saumbody she new."

"Fair enough, what's the story with these addresses so?" I asked innocently. (Having already scanned the piece of paper, I found it hard to believe that the spoilt WASP daughter of some Bush-loving former Enron executive would know people living in the locations listed therein.)

"Well friend, confidentially, this young lady has bin somewhat troublesome in the past and is saumthang of a rebel. Associatin' with the wrong kind, smokin' pot, drinkin', that sort of thang. Her parents, ah, believe she may have taken to walkin' the streets to support herself."

Oh well that's just lovely, I thought. You're an uppity little fraternity bitch exercising your right to make your parents' lives a living hell and they assume you're on the game because you disappear with no visible means of support. Maybe if Mr and Mrs Corporate America had devoted a little more time to effective and supportive parenting by watching some Oprah reruns, they wouldn't be in this little pickle. But what the hey, like I give a shit. Here was me dying to go home an hour after I'd started and then fate throws me a lifeline in the form of this nutter. I'm game for a laugh.

"Right, I see," I said. "And you want to check out these locations and see what turns up, yeah?"

Wayne nods his head slowly, silently marvelling I suspected, at my ability to assimilate information quickly and formulate a coherent strategy, a quality I believe is lacking in your average American.

"You got it friend. I got these here addresses offa contact of mine – we kinda share information in this binness – and I reckon they're as good a place to start as any. I have a car with me here in Dublin, but I figure I can get through this a lot quicker with the help of a guy like you who knows the cidy. I'll be happy to look after you real well for your time."

Shit. Now I regretted putting the meter on. Could have charged him the "specialist services" rate and fleeced him. Still, I'll figure something out as we go along.

"Right so," I said, "you want to get going and head to the first one?"

"Yes siree, lead the way." Wayne, Texas Ranger buckles up and we head out across the prairie, I mean down Chatham Street.

Location number one on the list was a dingy lane up behind the Ilac Centre. Actually had to get the map out for it. Grid reference 36 D4, and then it wasn't even listed it was so obscure. Just a number, so I had to check the index at the back of the bible, but there it was. This was a few years ago now, before all that Celtic Tiger bullshit allegedly rejuvenated this kip, and it was fairly dodgy around there. Hoped Wayne was "packing heat", 'cos I sincerely doubted I was covered for knife wounds under the terms of the critical illness policy I had somewhat presciently instigated with the union a few weeks previously.

So over the bridge and up O'Connell Street we go. Around the corner, past the Parnell Mooney – a lively spot to go for a pint by all accounts – and down past the back of the Ilac. (Can't divulge the exact location we were headed for, in case it's changed hands in the last while and the current owners take umbrage at the inference, however accurate, that their building was once the location of a knocking shop, and haul me into the Four Goldmines for a libel case.) I cruise down the lane, turn off, sorry, "kill" the engine and instinctively switch off the lights. I look at Wayne and nod towards a fairly dilapidated looking building.

"That's it there."

Wayne nods his head and looks around slowly, as if he could sense whether this was the place or not.

"Ahm gonna check it out. Be right back," Wayne drawled, and out he gets.

Maith an fear I thought to myself. A laugh's a laugh, but I had three bank managers depending on my continued use of my physical faculties and there was no way I was checking the place out. He walks towards the door and pauses to look up before banging on the door. Thought I should have swung the car around before I stopped so as to be ready for a quick getaway, should the need arise. No answer. Wayne gives it a minute and then gets back in the car. The words "thorough" and "not very" came to mind, but I said nothing. He was a "professional" after all.

"No joy?" I enquired.

"Doesn't seem to be much of anythang goin' on here tonight my friend. What say we head on to the nex one?"

Pulled a quick three-point turn and we're gone, headed for den of iniquity number two. Now this next place was definitely a knocking shop. In this game, a knowledge of the location of such facilities is required in order to best serve the needs of particular clients, be they farmers up for the match who haven't seen so much as a naked thigh since they had a roll in the top field with Rosaleen after the Queen of the Lakes festival in 1953, or visiting state dignitaries and businessmen who view the procurement of such services as perfectly normal conduct for people such as themselves who simply haven't the time to cultivate meaningful relationships with educated, dynamic and articulate young ladies.

So I shoot down Capel Street, over Grattan Bridge, up behind the Castle and on to Bride Street. Up past the Meath and cut across on to Camden Street. I stopped, gave Wayne a nod and gestured down a lane.

"There you go, Wayne."

"This it? OK. Won't be long."

He checks the number on the piece of paper and hops out. I move up a bit so I can keep an eye on proceedings. He strolls down the lane and knocks on the door. A curtain twitches upstairs and a minute later the door opens. After exchanging pleasantries, the bauld Wayne steps inside and the door closes.

Jesus, wait until I tell the lads this one. They'll have a field day with it.

About fifteen minutes later, Wayne emerges and tips his hat at the hooker inside who is careful not to show her face to the outside world. He gets back in the car and nods his head satisfactorily.

"OK, made some progress there," he says.

I bet you did I was thinking, though it didn't say much for his stamina.

"Oh yeah? What's the story?"

Wayne nods in the direction of the lane.

"Well she reckons that if our target was in the business, she might not yet be working in an established place such as this? Maw likely to be on the streets."

(A couple of things. First, I wasn't sure I was comfortable with the "our" target bit. I was just along for the ride, if you pardon the pun. And second, the whole American rising intonation thing, as illustrated by my use of the question mark, was beginning to get on my tits.)

"Maybe we should check out sum o' the places where the street girls hang out?"

Checking my watch, I figured it was a bit early for them to be out, but acquiesced to the request.

"Yeah, sure thing. There's three or four places they work from. We can do a quick tour and see what's going on."

"Sounds good. Let's go."

On the move again. Down to Wilton Place, along Percy Place around the Pepper Cannister, and back up to Fitzwilliam Square. Not a one out. Knew it was too early. Went over to the Maxol garage on Mespil Road, ostensibly to buy smokes. But in reality I was checking to see if there were any of them around the area. They sometimes use the pay phone nearby to arrange pick-ups with regulars when they have no credit on their phones.

Nothing happening at all – it's still only half nine. I explain the vagaries of the Dublin vice scene to Wayne and we elect to head to the third place on his list. Now this place I knew as well. It was a retail emporium specialising in the sale of quality adult erotic merchandise – books, videos, gels, accessories, poppers, you name it. A lot of these places were merely fronts for the really profitable side of the business – the vice proper. (My lawyer has advised me to say here that I am not suggesting for one second that this particular establishment, or indeed any one of the raft of such businesses that have popped up in Dublin in recent years, was, or is, in any way whatsoever involved in the prostitution business, and I am happy to clarify this point. It's complete horseshit, but I am nonetheless happy to clarify it.)

So I park outside and Wayne does his thing. Door opens and in he goes.

What was he really up to though? Call me a cynic, but I didn't really buy the Magnum PI thing. Where were his sidekicks? I mean, Magnum never solved a case without the help of Rick's shady contacts or TC's chopper. Something didn't add up. Maybe Wayne was just a sad, lonely delusional guy from the US who was over here playing out some big shot fantasy PI role? Was that a crime? No. A little wacko maybe, but pretty tame in the context of what some people do for kicks. Competitive curling for instance.

A good half hour later Wayne emerges from the premises, once again tipping his hat to his host as he leaves. He gets back in the car, looking a little disgruntled I have to say.

"Let's go see if any these whoars are out on the street yet."

After ten now, good and dark, and the ladies are out. No disrespect, but the majority of the girls who work the streets are no oil paintings. Good looking, fit, gamey types can afford to stay in their nice centrally located apartments, stick an ad in *In Dublin* and let the punters come to them. Well, they could until Mike Hogan got his arse kicked over allegedly letting them do just that, but you know what I mean. The howlers, on the other hand, have to stand under a lamppost and take what comes their way. Which on this particular night was a now sour-looking, fat Texan who looked like he just came last in a Garth Brooks look-alike competition. On Wilton Place I spotted one under forty and pulled up just in front of her. Wayne gets out and starts his little patter. Wish he'd get on with it. He was beginning to bug me now. Hadn't said a word since Rathmines and I had come to the conclusion that he was just another nutter living out a fantasy.

Now I just wanted to get him back to the hotel, get my money and go off and bring regular Dublin assholes home.

The back door opens and the hooker gets in.

"Howiya?" says your one.

"Alright?" I reply.

"He alrigh' is 'e?" she asks.

"Ah yeah, I reckon so."

Wayne gets back in the front and gives instructions.

"Okay, this young lady is gonna help me out, reckons she spoke to our target couple days ago. We're gonna have a talk aboud it back at the hotel."

Yeah right. I take off anyway for the Westbury. Pull up outside and the hooker gets out. Wayne gets out the wallet. Meter's reading about fifty quid. Before I can give the "specialist services" line, he peels off a ton and hands it to me. That'll do nicely.

"Now sir, that's for you. Much appreciate your help. Could you possibly give me your mobil fone number so I can call you later on to come pick this girl up when we're done?"

"Yeah, okay, hang on a second," I said.

I scribbled my mobile number down on a receipt and gave it to Wayne. He puts it in his wallet and tips his hat at me.

"Much obliged friend. You take care now."

"Will do. Good luck with the case Wayne," I say with a wry smile, nodding in the direction of the hooker, hoping that he might crack under the pressure of my witty inference and concede that all he was looking for all this time was a hooker. But no, he keeps it up.

"Thankee, ahm sure it'll work out."

I head off and do a bit of cruising around, very happy with my hundred pounds for a couple of hours work. Still nothing happening so I park up outside Spar on Baggot Street and continue with my reading material.

About two hours later, my phone rings as I'm coming down the dualler past the Montrose. No caller id at this time, so I didn't know who it was.

"Hello?"

"Howiya, Wayne said ye'd givus a lift if I rang ye."

"Oh right, yeah. You're at the Westbury still, are you?"

"Yeah."

"Right, I'll be outside in ten minutes."

"Righ', tanks."

Now I'd see what the crack was. I'd had enough hookers in my car over the years to know when they're going to or coming from a trick. Going to a job, they'd be reading the address off a scrap of paper, hardly a close friend's house. Or you might hear them on the phone telling someone where it was for security reasons, and saying they should be back within the hour. Coming from was a cinch. They'd be feeling like shit and would invariably ask if they could smoke. I always let them, because firstly it wasn't my car and I didn't give a shit if they burnt the seat covers, and secondly, I reckoned they needed it. But the dead giveaway was always when you dropped them back down to Baggot Street or wherever, and they were getting the money out. They would always only have a twenty-pound note. Four twenties makes eighty, standard price for a shag back then. And Wayne certainly had a nice roll on him when he was sorting me out after our recon mission.

I pull outside the Westbury and there she is, sucking on a cigarette.

Maybe.

"Howiya. Baggot Stree' please."

Off we go and I check her out in the mirror. She looks like shit, just staring out the window.

"He's a bit weird dat fella, issen 'e?" she says after a while.

"American. You know the way," I reply, not wanting to get too involved.

We arrive at the bridge and I stop and total the meter. Three pound forty plus forty pence unsocial hours plus one pound twenty pick-up charge makes a fiver.

"Now, that's a fiver please," I said.

"I've owney got twenty, alrigh?" she says.

Definitely.

Fairytale of Dublin

Friday before Christmas, 2001. Say no more. Every gobshite in the city decides to go for a drink after work. How pleasant. Only one wasn't enough and they all decided to get absolutely rat arsed and fall out of the pub at two in the morning.

It had been a very messy night, but mad busy so I wasn't complaining. Well I was, I always do, but you know what I mean. Anyway it was about five am, the work was all mopped up and I was thinking of heading home. Heard a call on the radio for a car for the centre and shouted in. Thought it might be an airport job, someone heading away early. No. Smithfield, a bird going over to Ballsbridge. That'll do nicely all the same, get me finished and off home out the dualler.

So I swing over the river and up Church Street, hang a left and rattle over the cobbles. Pull up outside the Jameson whiskey museum and buzz the apartment. The usual response – "on the way down". Sure you are. I know punters all over the city curse taxi drivers for being late most of the time and rightly so, but the reverse holds as well. If I take a radio job, I make it my business to be there on time – I don't want some narky git chewing my ear off for being late. And by the same token, I would appreciate it when I get to a job if the punter in question makes it their business to get into the car as quickly as possible, and generally when you hear them saying "on the way down", it means they're not ready and not on their way down.

A whole eight minutes later, and still no sign of her. Sod it, put the meter on. If she's going to hold me up she can pay for it. Then I see this old guy shuffling towards me along the path. He looks to be in rag order, one hand on the wall to hold himself up, the other one on his trousers, to hold them up by the looks of it. It's fairly cold out and he's making slow progress to wherever he's headed. Finally, my passenger deigns to join me, boyfriend in tow to see her off. He opens the door to the car for her, gives her a kiss, and then notices the old lad by the railings.

"Are you alright?" he calls over to him.

The old lad pauses and looks around, trying to locate the friendly voice. The boyfriend trots across the cobbles towards him.

"Hello there, are you alright?" he asks again.

"I'm just trying to get back to my accommodation," the old lad says, in an unexpectedly well spoken voice.

"Where is it? Do you need a hand?"

Inwardly applauding the decency of my passenger's boyfriend, I switch off the meter and get out of the car.

"What's up?" I ask.

"Good evening sir," the old lad says to me. "I'm just trying to make my way home to my accommodation. Do you know the hostel quite near here?"

"I do yeah, the one on Benburb Street?"

"That's the one. Is it much further?" he asked.

"Would you like a lift?" the boyfriend inquired. "You don't mind, do you?" he then asked me.

"No, not at all, fine by me."

With that, my passenger and her boyfriend helped the old lad into the front seat of the car. He then joins her in the back and I head on down Bow Street towards the hostel on Benburb Street.

"This is very kind of you I must say," the old lad says politely as he settled himself in. "And of you too, young lady. Forgive me for not turning around but I can't turn my head terribly well ... I was ... mugged last week on my way back from the post office by two gougers after my pension ..."

"Oh my God, that's terrible," the girl said in what seemed to be an Aussie accent. "Were you hurt?"

"Well, they roughed me up a bit ... which at my age doesn't take too long!" he replied, making light of the incident, but the faltering tone of his voice told a different story. "Pushed me to the ground when they got what they were looking for, broke my glasses," he said, gently fingering his now sellotaped frames. "I'm getting a new pair on Monday from an opticians in town. The optometrist there is an old friend of mine."

"And how long are you ... in the hostel, do you mind me asking?" she said.

"Almost a year now," he said. "I lived in Clontarf for thirty-eight years, in a lovely house with my dear wife Elizabeth. I had a small business over in the northside, but a couple of years ago it went bankrupt and I lost everything. I'd been struggling for a while, but I didn't know anything else and tried to keep going as best I could, but it all got too much for me in the end, and it went into liquidation. It was a great shock to Lizzy, as you can imagine. You get accustomed to a certain standard of living over time and then, whoosh, it's all gone in the space of a week. Then they came after me for my house to settle the debts. It was a terrible time really. Lizzy couldn't take the stress of it anymore ... she died of a heart attack a few months later, poor thing ..."

"Oh that's so sad, I'm sorry," the girl says, "and ... do you, have any family?"

"I do yes, a son. He lives in Australia now, has done for years. We don't really get along I'm afraid. Melbourne he's in. And is that an Australian accent you have yourself?" he says smiling.

"I'm from New Zealand actually," she replies in a friendly tone. "I have some friends in Melbourne though, it's really nice there. Have you been over to visit them at all?"

"No, no, not at my age, I couldn't face the journey. Don't think I'd be a very welcome guest somehow. He was home for the funeral alright, but didn't stay around too long."

I was parked outside the door of the hostel at this stage, but didn't want to cut your man off. He was probably delighted to have someone to talk to who was interested in what he was saying. He stops then and looks awkwardly at us, me first and then the two passengers in the back, before cracking a faint smile and clapping one hand on his leg.

"Right then, here we are, home, safe and sound," he says ironically. "A very goodnight to you, my dear, and thank you once again for the lift. It was very kind of you."

As the boyfriend hops out to give him a hand getting out of the car, he turns himself around a little to give her a smile and winks at her saying, "I hope Santa brings you something nice," nodding his head in the direction of her beau. She smiles warmly at him, and wishes him all the best. I went on ahead to buzz the intercom so he wouldn't be standing around in the cold. He climbs the few steps slowly, resting both feet on each one before tackling the next, the way little kids do when they are first mastering the art of stair climbing. As the porter opens the door to let him in, he turns around to thank us once more before going inside. The young lad then sticks his head in the back of the car to say he'll walk back to the apartment.

"Text me when you get home," he says, kissing her lightly on the cheek.

"Will do, love you, bye," she replies.

I swing the car around, make an illegal right turn on to Blackhall Place and get back on to the quays, heading for my original destination. Passing over Queen Street bridge, I flick the meter back on. All's quiet in the car as we go down the quays towards Butt bridge. I like driving around the city at this time, between five and six am. All the revellers are gone home and the rest of the city hasn't yet woken up to face another day in the life. Just taxis scooting around the deserted streets, accompanied by a few delivery guys making the most of the early hours to get their city centre drops out of the way before the inevitable gridlock resumes.

I felt really bad for the old guy back at the hostel. He wasn't pissed at all. He'd had a few, and God knows he probably needed them. It was just the way he was walking with his hand against the railing, it looked like he was locked. To my jaded eyes he was just another piss artist wino shuffling home, no different to any of the other dozen or so such characters I'd see any night of the week. And in reality he was a gent, obviously came from good stock, and did well for himself originally but had now fallen on hard times and ended up in a hostel.

"He was some guy, wasn't he?" my passenger finally said.

"Yeah, he was, really sound. Unreal the way things have turned out for him though, isn't it? You just don't know ..."

"Fuck yeah, I mean, you work hard all your life, you raise your family, and just when you should be able to kick back and enjoy your twilight years, you lose it all, including your wife. Jesus, that sucks ... and to end up there in a bloody hostel, like, relying on charity for shelter ... and at Christmas, Jesus ... and he was such a dear, sweet old man ..."

At this point she wasn't talking to me at all, she was thinking out loud.

"Whereabouts in Ballsbridge do you want?" I said, cutting across her monologue.

"Ahm, I'm on Claremont Road, thanks."

"No problem," I said, swinging left onto Lansdowne Road and over the tracks.After a minute or so, she asks me how I get along with my father.

"As best I can, you know?" I replied, trying to be as non-committal as possible. Be here all night if we started in on that one.

"Yeah ... shit, you know something?" she continued, "I came over here about three months ago, and before I left, I had the worst row with my dad. He didn't want me to leave at all. I met Brian, my boyfriend – the guy back there – when he was in Oz, yeah? I was visiting friends in Melbourne and just met him one night in the pub, you know? But we really clicked, like straight away. Hung out constantly for three weeks or something. He even let his mates go back to Sydney without him and we went travelling ourselves for a week, it was awesome. Anyway, he had to go back home, and then, about two months after he left, he rang me one day, totally out of the blue, and asked me to come to Ireland. I was stunned, but psyched as well, you know? Couldn't get him out of my head at all. Sounds really corny I know, but that's the way it was ... Anyway, my dad totally flipped when I told him I was going, giving up a good job, going half way round the world to some guy you've only known a few weeks, all that sort of stuff. So we had this huge row, and he wouldn't speak to me at all. You see, my mum died when I was little, and I have like four brothers, so I was his little princess ... he knew that I really wanted to go, and he knew why, he just didn't want to me to go, for my own sake, in case it didn't work out and I'd be here all on my own, you know? So I left really early one morning, my brother drove me to the airport and I never really said goodbye, to, my dad ..."

She was holding back the tears at this stage, and her voice was really uneven. Normally I couldn't care less what kind of alleged personal traumas people in my car claim to be going through, but she was sound, really genuine, and family-related stuff is different anyway, it really at eats at people, or at least it should. About half way down Claremont Road she mumbled,

"Just here, thanks," and I pulled in to the kerb.

"Yeah, I know what you're saying ... but everybody's different you know?" I said, throwing in my tuppence worth on life. "You can't expect to see eye to eye with people all the time, or for them to agree with you all the time either. Now, most of the time I just say fuck it and do my own thing anyway, but family's different, you know? You can't choose them, which is crap, so you just have to make the most of it and sort things out. The longer you leave it though, the worse it gets. When things fester like that, people get really stubborn, and it's really hard to sort shit out, you know?"

"Tell me about it ... you're right though, it's really hard the longer it goes on. I don't know, just seeing that guy there tonight really brought it home to me again. I don't know why, the situations are totally different, I suppose it's just that ... oh fuck it, I don't know, I'm talking shit now," she said, straightening herself up in the seat and opening her bag to get her wallet out. "How much do I owe you?"

As I give her her change, she perks up and smiles at me. "Do you know what time it is?"

"It's twenty to six," I say.

"Great," she says affirmatively, "I'm gonna go in and ring my dad. Goodnight, and Happy Christmas!"

"Cheers, all the best," I reply as she gets out and trots up the driveway to her house.

I swing the car around and switch off my meter, giving a quick look back to make sure she gets in okay. Lovely arse on her by the way. *Maith an fear* Brian.

Off I go up the dualler to Bray, making a mental note to go back to the hostel in a day or so and give the old lad a bottle of whiskey and a few quid for the Christmas. I didn't of course, self-absorbed asshole that I am, but I meant to, if that counts for anything.

"I dun nuttin!"

unday the seventeenth of November, 2002. I was heading in to the cinema to see *Bowling for Colombine* at eight twenty. I'd meant to get out about four or so and do a bit before skiving off to the flicks, but didn't actually get my arse in gear until about seven. Did a few quick hops and then about quarter to eight decided to head in to town and get parked up. Shooting down through Harold's Cross I see a lad at the kerb with his hand up, rocking backwards and forwards in a steady fashion, concentrating hard to keep himself upright. Reckoned he was heading into town, so I pulled in. He trots towards the car and at the fifth attempt managed to secure adequate purchase on the handle to open the door. He pours himself into the car, belches, farts and then turns to me to issue instructions.

"Alright buddy? A1, A1. Dundrrrum pleaze, tank yew," he slurs at me.

Shite! Dun-bloody-drum, completely the opposite direction to what I wanted. Still, my own fault for stopping for him in the first place, so I bang on the meter and go for a u-turn at the hospice, which is no easy thing on that poxy road with constant traffic coming at you from every direction. A slight break in the traffic flow and I execute a fairly hairy but nonetheless successful turn, much to the consternation of my fellow motorists, whose irritation I dismiss with a few well chosen expletives, inwardly directing them at my passenger.

"Iss dat alright wit ye buddy? Not, takin' ye, out of yer way, am I?" he slurs at me, the exertion of constructing complete sentences causing him to close his eyes and concentrate hard, at the same time nodding his head, willing the words to come out in the intended sequence.

I mutter a few words of agreeable consent and put the foot down, as well as my window, welcoming the freezing cold air into the car as its circulation helps dissipate the foul stench of his ale-ridden exhalations.

Past the dog track I go, willing the lights at the junction of Leinster Road to remain green, so obviously they change to red. Regretting that I have not yet safely reached my PNR (Point of No Return, being that distance from the stop line when the resulting combination of certain elements, such as speed, weather conditions, number of morons in front of me who can't distinguish amber from red, and the probability of doughnut-eating cops being in a car at the junction in question, dictate whether or not I can make it through the lights), I reluctantly hit the brakes. My travelling companion takes the seemingly eternal stop at the lights to turn in my direction and size me up. Obviously content with what he sees, however scary that seemed to me in that it suggested to him we may have something in common, he nods his head slowly, and extends his paw.

"I'm Mmmichael, pleazzzed te meet ye buddy. Whatz yer own name, 'fye don't mind me askin?"

"Alan," I say curtly, shaking his hand as quickly as possible and then wiping my hand on my jeans.

"Verrry, pleazzezed te meet ye, Alan," he says, nodding his head rhythmically like one of those stupid dogs non-dog owners have wagging in the rear window of their cars for the amusement of their fellow motorists.

"Howz tings, Alan ... I mean, howz tings like, are ye busy? Ye, mmmakin' a few pound yeah? I know itz a tough ol' game, dis drivin' malarkey ..."

"Alright, you know, just doing my bit, that's all," I replied, trying to keep my response as simple as possible, for fear of launching him off on a tangent to an area of conversation which was currently way beyond the cognitive capacity of the 6cc motor engine driving his few remaining brain cells.

"I see, I see ... yeah, yeah. Feel frrree te tell me te shut up now 'fye like ... I'm jus' tryin' te make con-con-con-ver-sssation," he says, the multi-syllabic word putting a real strain on his mental resources.

There is nothing I would rather have done than tell him to shut the fuck up and stop annoying me, but from experience, it's always the wrong call, as those assholes who offer you the chance to terminate the inane con-con-con-ver-sssation they instigated are the very ones who would take the most umbrage if you justifiably elected to do so, and their alcohol-fuelled gibberish would swiftly turn into vitriolic paranoia. "Have I done something to offend you, have I?" they'd say. Or "What's your problem? Do you think you're better than me, is that it, yeah?" And then you're into another whole dimension of grief that you just don't need, so I reluctantly nodded once more and said, "You're alright."

A minute of blissful silence followed as I rolled over yet more recently laid ramps on Rathgar Avenue. Then Michael starts up again, rambling angrily to himself. "Fuckin' bitch ... ssstewpid fuckin' bitch, yeah well she can fuck off so if dat's whad she wants, see if I give a ffffuck ..."

"What's that?" I said, the whiff of scandal arousing my curiosity.

Michael turns solemnly to me, about to unleash his tale of woe, then pauses, and declines.

"Ah no, I cudden lay dat on ye buddy, d'ye know whad I mean?" he says, as if I'd be distraught on his behalf after hearing of the demise of his pathetic relationship. Now, I know I'm judgemental, and sometimes I think it's something I should try and temper and restrain, but I've met enough assholes in my life to know that when a bloke in my car is pissed and starts ranting to himself about his woman and what a bitch she is, chances are it's his fault that she eventually saw sense and told him to sling his hook.

"Go on, what did you do?" I said in a but-sure-aren't-we-all-just-lads-acting-the-maggot-getting-pissed-night-and-day-and-so-what-if-we-give-the-missus-a-slap-or-do-the-dirt-now-and-then-no-harm-done kind of voice, egging him on to spill the beans to a seemingly like-minded soul.

"I dun nuttin, I dun fffuckin' nuttin, I'm tellin' ye, dunno whad 'er bleedin' problim is, stewpid cow. Jaysus. In de boozer las' nite, big gang of us, lashin' inte de gargle. As ye do, Saterdey nite like, yeah? An' me mate's bird's sister – Sandra – was doin' de karaoke yeah? Givin' it lodes she was. Singin' rite bleedin' at me. Now mine wassen dere ye see, over at her ma's she was, narkin' on about me like she always bleedin' is, yeah? So I sees her goin' te de jax an' she's givin' me de mincers, bigtime, te folley 'er like, yeah? Now, fair enough, I shudden have righ', but, I was bleedin' gargled man, ye know yerself de way id is. So I folley her an' we go down the hall a bit te de where de payfone is. She's smilin' at me an' noddin' her head, ye know? So I launch in an' start wearin' de face off 'er, an' she's luvin' it, grabbin' at me lad an' all, de durty bitch. An' we're goin' ad it goodo when Anto comes down fer te go fer a piss, an' he bleedin' flips. Pulls her off me, gives me a smack like I was a bleedin' kid, an' starts roarin' at de tew of us. 'Course den her bleedin' sister comes down, de nosy bitch, starts stickin' 'er oar in, givin' me an earful. So I told her to go an' fuck 'erself, an' Anto loses de plot an' decks me, yeah? Now, I don't mind dat so much, 'cos he was fairly gargled himself an' probley didden mean it like, he's me mate, yeah? But still, poxy bouncers fucked me out and barred me. An' Anto's bird o'coarse goes spreadin' it round about whad I dun, exageratin' no end, fuckin' bitch, she's always stirrin' it up. Den me moth hears all aboud it dis mornin an' starts in at me, screamin' an' yellin'. So I split down de boozer dere after me lunch, had a few quiet pints, nobody boderin' me. But ye have te go home at some stage, so here I am. Jaysus, probly get anudder earful now when I go in … such a lode o' bollix, I'm telling ye man, ye've no idea. Are ye mmmarried yerssself, Alan, are ye?"

"No I'm not," I said emphatically, trying not to laugh out loud at the Snapper-like antics of this gobshite.

"Keep it dat way brudder, it's a lode o' bollix. Ye can't do antin' widout dere bein' a bleedin' row."

Heading down by The Dropping Well I ask him what part of Dundrum he wants.

"Strayed on buddy, strayed on."

So I go "strayed" on along the Milltown Road under the old railway bridge and then he changes the subject from alcohol fuelled infidelity and subsequent domestic acrimony to local history.

"Dat's de Nine Arches dere, righ'? And did yew know, did yew know dat at one time dere was a pub up my way called de Nine Arches?" he says earnestly.

"I did yeah, up in Windy Arbour."

"Dat is correct, dat is correct," he says, somewhat dismayed at the fact that I knew the answer to his question, like it was on a par with the tie-break question in the Mastermind grand final.

"Are ye local yerself, buddy?" Magnus then asks me, still reeling with incredulity, and suspecting that I would have to be from the locality to know such a thing.

I was actually originally from Dundrum, but wasn't going to tell him that in case he decided we were now best mates, on account of the fact that he had called me "buddy" about sixty-four times in the space of the last eight minutes.

"No, I'm not, I'm northside myself," I said, nearly choking at the utterance of such a falsehood. I fucking hate the northside, but will quite happily claim it as my domicile when it suits me.

"Northside, yeah? Verry good, verry good, fare play, A1 buddy, A1. I reckon ye're A1, d'ye know dat? Don't get me wrong like Alan, I know I don't know ye very well, bud I reckon ye're A1, d'ye know whad I'm sayin' te ye? Ye're a decent skin, same as meself, yeah? A1."

I was seriously tempted to stop the car and throw him face down on to the rocks in the Dodder river at the suggestion that we had anything remotely in common, but I let it slide on the grounds that he was pissed and I would more than likely never meet this particular asshole again. And such an act of manslaughter, justified or otherwise, would have wasted valuable time, and I had a movie to watch in approximately sixteen minutes.

"Now, d'ye see that car dere," he says, pointing at a BMW in front of me, "yew want te folley him yeah? Can ye do dat?"

I summon all my powers of concentration and with remarkably advanced hand-eye co-ordination for someone who's only been driving ten years, manage to negotiate my way into the right turn only lane and progress across the bridge on to the

Dundrum Road.

"Fare play buddy, A1, now strayed on up. I'm up near the lights at Taney, yeah?"

"Yeah, no problem," I said, tearing up the road towards Dundrum village.

"Dat's de pub dere, Alan. Dat's de pub dat used te be called de Nine Arches," Michael informs as we shoot through Windy Arbour.

"That's the one, yeah," I said wearily, now utterly drained of all desire to communicate.

"Yer left here now fer me Alan tanks, an' mind de ramps, dey'll make a bollix o' yer car," Michael says helpfully.

"Whereabouts do you want?"

"Ah, righ' here … strayed on, now a left … strayed on … an' jus' here, tank yew buddy. A1, A1."

Totalled the meter, €10.75.

"Now, that's a tenner please," I said, happily willing to forego the seventy-five cents if it meant getting him out of the car quicker.

"No problem buddy, no problem," Michael says, leaning perilously in my direction as he struggled to extricate a ten euro note from the deepest recesses of his trouser pockets.

"Now," he says, unrolling the note and holding it up to the light carefully to make sure he was only handing over one of them, "dere ye go, tank yew verrry much."

I take the note and once again reluctantly shake his proffered paw. Parting is such sweet sorrow.

"Ta, all the best," I offer as a farewell.

"An' yew buddy, an yew. A1, tanks for gettin' me home, alldough I dunno why I bleedin' bodered wit de yewmer she'll be in," he says nodding his dopey head in the direction of his house.

After what seemed like four hours of groping the door panel, he managed to locate the release handle and opened the door, grabbing the central pillars of the car to hoist himself into an upright position. He turned around to stick his head in the door for one last goodbye to his new buddy and finally shut the door. Into reverse before the door was closed, and off I went, checking the rearview mirror as I went to see if he had fallen down yet. No, he had managed to make it to a wall where he was now in the process of relieving himself, one arm outstretched against the wall to support himself and hopefully avoid a messy splashback from the pebble dashed surface.

Tore into town, threw the car up on the pavement beside The Long Stone, and hopped into the cinema where my real buddy was impatiently waiting for me to join him.

"Alright Paul, how's things?" I said cheerily.

"You're late. Alright, how are you?" he said.

"A1, A1."

The Comedian

Sunday night of the October bank holiday weekend and the streets are hopping. Everyone who hasn't gone to Galway or Kilkenny to get pissed has decided that they are not going to sit indoors when they could be out getting drunk, delirious in the knowledge that they can suffer with a hangover the following day and not have to pretend they are working. Things had been ticking along nicely and then about midnight I got a fare out to Killinarden in Tallaght. That was that, I'd be out there for the next few hours doing local hops. I'd always heard that Sundays are a good night to go out up there. People who didn't have jobs to get up for in the morning obviously didn't give a shit about being hung over, and those who did have jobs to get up for were happy to suffer the pain of a hang-over if it gave them another chance to maybe score with someone in a similar position.

Dropped off in Killinarden and shot back down to the village where I got three birds coming out of Fables who were heading down to another pub nearby. They weren't in the cart six seconds when out came the deodorants, blushers, mascara, brushes, mirrors, foundation, lipstick and God knows what else is required by women these days to hide their real appearance from unsuspecting suitors. The conversation, to which I was not an invited contributor, concerned itself with a serious discussion of the merits of the revolutionary Revo hair styler, a new device which apparently facilitated the modern woman in now having to spend one hour getting ready in the morning instead of two and a half. And all for the unbelievable-once-in-a-lifetime-not-available-in-the-shops price of €64.95 plus €9.95 postage and packing. The girls pronounced it "fuckin' deadly" and "well wurt de money" so who am I to argue? It must be "fuckin' deadly". We did the money thing and off they went, totally unrecognisable from the three girls who sat into my car some six minutes ago.

They were only out of the car when a young lad comes lurching towards the car and hops in the front seat, grinning sheepishly to himself. "Alrigh' bud, just goin' down te Crumlin please, yeah?" he says.

"No problem," I replied, swinging the car around quickly. Your man seemed sound enough, so I initiated conversation as I negotiated the poxy ramps on Wellington Lane.

"What's the crack? Many in there tonight is there?"

"Oh yeah, it's bleedin' jammers, man. Slawter in dere now, big mill 'tween me mates an' anudder team from our league."

"Oh yeah, what happened?" I asked. I love hearing about and seeing fights, and am constantly amazed to hear how they can be the makings of a memorable night out for those involved, and indeed, sometimes the actual reason for going out to a particular venue in the first place.

"I dunno really … well yeah I do ackshully, me mate kinda started it. He's gargled – so am I – but that's why we went out. He's off te Australia for a year in de mornin' so we've bin on a bender for de whole weekend, ye know? We were owney havin' a laugh, started slaggin' dem 'cos we hockeyed dem las' week. Three nil, away an' all, fuckin' deadly it was. So den one o' dem fucks a bottle at me mate, nearly took 'is bleedin' eye out. So he jumped on yer man an' started punchin' de head off him, I jumped on anudder lad, started punchin' de head off him, before ye know it, I'm fucked out on me ear, an' dey're all let stay in. Load o' bollix, 'cos tonite was me first nite allowed back in dere, I've been barred fer six monts, an' now I'm barred agen. Fuck it ..."

"Where'll you go now?" I asked him.

"Back up te de fuckin' Playhouse I s'pose. Alrigh if I smoke?"

I nod in acquiescence and he lights up his cigarette. On the radio the newscaster reveals that a young lad shot in Crumlin the previous night has died in hospital.

My passenger shakes his head ruefully, musing out loud on the insanity of the increasing amount of gun-related crime in this shitty city.

"Fuck's sake man, people shootin' each udder fer nuttin' dese days, mental innit? A couple o' years ago, someone pisses ye off or robs yer car or whatever, ye goes up to 'im an' ye beat de head off 'im. Now, it's all bleedin' guns, gobshites blowin' each udder's head off for the littlest ting. Me mate Philo," he says, gesturing back towards the location of the melee in the pub, "he got shot 'bout a year ago. Some bloke lookin' fer the lad dat stole 'is motor arrives up at de green 'round our way. Sees Philo sittin' on de wall wid 'is mates and goes over to 'im, starts moutin' off aboud 'im robbin' 'is poxy car. Philo tells 'im te fuck off an' yer man pulls out a shooter and shoots 'im in de bleedin' face. Had te get reconstruction surgery dun on 'is gob, in bits 'e was. Wassen even him an' all, muppet can't even drive, fer fuck's sake ..."

At this point I'm heading down Captain's Road and suddenly some moron reverses out of their driveway really fast, not looking to see if there is anything coming that might legitimately impede their egress. I swerve to avoid the car and blast my horn at them.

"Fuckin' asshole," my passenger roars out the window at them, saving me the trouble of doing so.

"Bet ye dat wuz a bird doin' dat, tick bitch. Useless bleedin' drivers dey are, aren't dey?"

Now fair's fair, I'm not chauvinistic at all, but, in my experience, women do account for a greater proportion of the morons on our roads who are terrifyingly incapable of handling a mechanically-propelled vehicle in the manner in which they were intended for. Plenty of men are crap drivers too, don't get me wrong, it's just that there are more crap women drivers out there than men. Men probably cause more accidents through speeding than women, but women do tend to do more stupid things on the roads. If the observation skills they utilise so effectively when shopping during the sales could be deployed in the same fastidious fashion whilst they are driving, I reckon the roads would be a lot safer. Classic example: rearview mirror angled downwards so as to aid the application of make up on the way to work, on the way home from work, on the way to the gym, on the way into town, etc. etc. Or my own personal favourite, wing mirrors permanently in the retracted position so they can squeeze their gigantic Fiestas and Polos into parking spaces designed to accommodate much smaller cars like Chrysler Voyagers or Land Rovers.

"Yeah, they are, crap," I concur agreeably with him as I hang a left off Stanaway Road as instructed.

"I had me ma's car de udder nite, yeah? Down in me mate's gaf havin' a few cans watchin' the footie. His sister goes out te park her Micra out on the road fer de mornin' 'cos de aul lad goes te work before her, yeah? Now I wuz parked along de kerb, loads o' room fer her to ged out, cuda got a bleedin' bus out, never mind a poxy Micra. Next ting, all I hear is bang, an' in she comes roarin' cryin' – after hittin' me auld one's car a smack. So I goes out te have a look and dere's dey arse o' her yoke wedged inte de bonnet of me auld dear's Vento! 'How'd ye do dat ye fuckin' eejit?' I says. An' d'ye know whad she says te me? 'Me foot slipped!'"

He was a great story teller and I was cracking up laughing at the incident, but he wasn't done yet, and delivers the tail end of the story with considerable aplomb and impeccable timing as I pull outside his house, where in the driveway, sits a new silver Vento with a smashed-up light cluster, colour-coded bumper and bonnet. He sits forward in his seat, nodding his head earnestly to assure me of the veracity of the story.

"So I look down ad 'er feet, an' d'ye know what she's wearin'? Poxy bleedin' slippers! I swear te God! Slippers! I ask ye! Big bleedin' furry yokes dey were an' all, fuckin' rabbit's ears and whiskers on dem, de lot!

"'So dat's why dey're called slippers?' I seys to 'er an' she's off agen roarin'. Den her aul fella comes out an' sees de mess an' he starts in ad 'er fer bein' a tick cow. Oh, fuck's sake, pantomime it wuz, ye wudden ged it wit Laurel and bleedin' Hardy man!"

I was creased up laughing at his animated expressions and impersonations of his mate's sister roaring crying in her pjs and bunny slippers in the driveway, her little car embedded into the front of the Vento.

"So dat's her insurance fucked, can ye imagine her fillin' out the claim fer dat? Dey'd be wettin' demselves in PMPA readin' dat dey wud. Fuck's sake … well dat's all from me fer de nite, you've bin a great audience, ye really have. How much is dat bud?" he says, reaching for his wallet.

I give him a discount for entertainment value, but he won't hear of it and tops up the fare with a generous tip before getting out of the car. He was great crack, and a decent fella too, despite his proclivity for violence in night clubs.

"How'm I supposed to get home?"

Thursday night, some time around May or June of this year, finds me up in Leopardstown. I normally only go up there on a Friday or Saturday night when it's absolutely hopping, but there was a huge crowd up there this night on account of it being the night the exams in UCD had ended, and tomorrow's elite were on the piss in Blackrock all day and had continued their revelling in Club 92.

I had already got a quick hop from there down to Cabinteely so I shot back up for another fare. You can get some right assholes up there so I usually pull up at the ATM and if anyone asks me if I'm free, I tell them I'm waiting for someone. I then suss them out and if they look alright, I tell them that my intended occupants are late and they can get in. This normally gets things off to a good start in my opinion, because the punters are grateful they have got a taxi instead of all the other people milling around and they are less likely to give you too much shit.

So there I am, turning people away like a bouncer at Lillie's on a Saturday night, when I see three absolutely gorgeous looking chicks heading my way. They'll do nicely I say to myself. Not harbouring any dishonourable intentions you understand, just figured they'd be hassle-free and nice to look at for a few minutes instead of three sweaty rugby jocks talking shite about all the birds in there who were gagging for it and how they could've scored if they wanted to. I was so taken with the ladies that I didn't notice until it was too late some bloke had gone around the other side of the car, opened the back door and slumped down on the seat, shouting, "C'mon lads, I've got one!" as he did so.

I whip around to see this preppy little shit, all of twenty-one, flaked out on the back seat.

"What's up with you?" I shouted at him. "Where do you think you're going?"

He looks up at me, utterly dumbfounded by the stupidity of my question. "Home, man, Mount Merrion, yeah? Hang on a sec, there's two more coming now."

No sign of anyone joining him so I tell him to sod off, that he's pissed and I'm not taking him home in the state he's in.

"Relax man, I'm not drunk," he says, sobering up momentarily at the prospect of being kicked out of the car, totally aware that nobody else will take him home.

"Where are your mates then?" I bark at him.

He looks around the car and then outside for a second, shrugs his shoulders and says, "Fuck them so, I'm going home. Mount Merrion ... please."

"Whereabouts in Mount Merrion?" I ask, trying to get the exact details out of him before he falls asleep.

"The church, 'side Kiely's, that's fine."

Meanwhile, the three honeys have got into another taxi, so I reluctantly start the meter and move off. Down through Sandyford Industrial Estate, down the hill, quick left and a quick right onto South Avenue. Over the ramps and through the little roundabout down to the church. Not a word said between us as yet. I stop at the entrance to the church car park and quickly total the meter.

"Now, that's €6.80," I say curtly, turning around.

He's still slumped on the back seat so I give him a shove, and start shouting "Oi!" at him. He starts mumbling some shite so I turn the radio up full blast.

"What? What the fuck?" he says, startled into an upright position.

"You said the church. Here we are. That's €6.80 please. Come on, get your shit together, I haven't got all night."

"Yeah, relax man, yeah?" he says, looking around the unfamiliar surroundings. "Where're the lads?"

"I don't know and I don't care. You got into the taxi on your own and said the church in Mount Merrion. Now here we are, so quit fucking around and give me the money."

"Chill man. Jesus, what's your problem?"

"You're my problem. I haven't got time for this shit, now hurry up."

He pulls himself together somewhat and opens the door to get out. He staggers to his feet and reaches into his jacket for his wallet. At this stage, I've got a bad feeling about this one, so I put on the hand brake and take off my seat belt. Sure enough, he staggers around for a minute at the front passenger door, pretending to be taking out a note, then mutters something incomprehensible, turns around and casually walks off into the night. Unbelievable. I hop out of the car and trot after him.

"Oi, where do you think you're going, asshole?" I shout at him.

"Who're you calling an asshole?" he says, turning around casually.

"You, moron. You owe me €6.80 for your taxi fare. Now cop the fuck on and give it to me, alright?"

"How'm I supposed to get home?"

At this stage, the south county UCD frat boy superiority complex sets in, and he gives me a snide my-daddy's-a-partner-in-KPMG kind of look.

"What money? I don't owe you any money. The lads are paying for it. I got the taxi on the way up ..."

"Listen moron," I said slowly, my patience wearing extremely thin, "you were in my taxi on your own. You owe me the money. I don't give a shit who paid for the taxi up to Club 92. You owe me the fare for the way home, so cop on."

"You cop on," he says to me.

Now I knew I was dealing with a complete asshole. "You cop on." What kind of moronic response is that? It's like something a four-year-old would say, and it actually reminded me of an incident a few months previously where some idiot had pulled out into the bus lane at Ossory Road bridge in North Strand without looking to see if there was anything coming. And there was – me, whipping down the bus lane back into town. Had to stand on the brakes to avoid rear-ending the stupid cow. At the next lights, I got out, strolled up to her car and banged on the window. She opens the window and I berate her for being a moron, closing with "Learn how to drive." And, unable to come up with a justifiable riposte because she knew she was totally in the wrong, she says, "You learn how to drive!" Anyway, to paraphrase one of Denis Farina's many classic lines in *Midnight Run*, back to moron number two.

"Look, you owe me €6.80," I said, trying to break it down for him. "I don't care if the lads were supposed to pay it, they're not here. If you don't have it, we'll go up to your house and you can get it, okay? Just stop pissing me around or I'll deck you, I'm warning you, I don't need this shit."

Now, as the contents of one of the other chapters of this book will illustrate, I have had runners before, and it's no big deal really in the great scheme of things, but this one was different. For a start, it could never have been a runner, given the state this sap was in; he could barely walk. And it wasn't about the money – bad and all as things are, I thankfully don't need to worry about where my next €6.80 is coming from. It was his attitude that really bugged me, as if living in some huge detached house in Mount Merrion gave him diplomatic immunity, some kind of *carte blanche* to do as he pleased, and to hell with the little people.

"Oh yeah, you will, will you?" he says, goading me.

So, at the risk of incriminating myself, I did. Well, I didn't actually deck him, I shoved him backwards, the way kids used to do in school as their peers shouted "A! G! A,G,R! A,G,R,O! AGRO!" It was a right shove though, and he fell over, as was intended. It had the desired effect, and by the time he managed to pick himself up, he had sobered up to quite a large degree.

"Alright, man, take it easy, yeah?" he mumbled somewhat contritely. "I'll get you the money. We'll have to go around to my house though."

"That's what I suggested, dickhead. Now get in the car," I said firmly.

We walk back to the car and I escort him into the front seat, just in case he decides to make another break for freedom. As I reverse out of the car park, I ask him where he lives. He gives me a house number and a road name very near to where we were. So, I drive around the corner and turn on to the appointed road, stopping outside the house.

"Go on," I said, "go in and get the money, and hurry up. I'm getting sick of this shit."

He doesn't move, just turns around and gives me a big dopey smile.

"That's not my house man. I don't live here, I live up in Foxrock …"

"Well why did you ask me to take you down here in the first place then?"

"Dunno man, dunno."

"Fair enough," I said, flicking the car into reverse to turn around, "I know where we'll go to sort this out."

"What are you doing man? Where are you going?" he says, suddenly alarmed at the possibilities opened up by my open-ended statement.

Now much as I would like to have brought him up to Kilternan or somewhere and thrown him down a disused lead mine shaft, I figured my best option would be to go down to the cops and let them sort it out, so I headed for the dualler and Blackrock garda station.

"You won't pay me what you owe me, you're pissing me off and you're wasting my time. I've had enough of this shit, so we're going down to the cop shop in Blackrock and see what they have to say."

The realisation that I wasn't kidding around jolted him somewhat, and he starts yabbering about how sorry he was, and how he'd go in and get the money and blah blah blah, but at this point I wasn't listening to him anymore.

Quarter to three finds us in the lobby of the well-appointed Blackrock garda station. A young cop comes out to deal with the situation. I give him the details and one look at the moron I have in tow confirms the validity of my predicament to him.

"Hello? What's your name?" the cop asks him sternly.

He mumbles his name incoherently, and much as I would like to tell you what it was, and where he lived, and what he looked like, my generally accommodating but understandably cautious solicitor has advised me to omit such details, in case the sap decides to sue me for defamation of some sort. I pointed out that the records of the incident in question could be made available to us in the event of such an action, and thus we could rely on truth as our defence and be declared victors in the court, but it was then pointed out to me that, sometimes, you can't afford to win a case, because the other side wouldn't have a penny to their name, so you have no chance of even recovering your own legal costs from them, never mind receiving your constitutionally awarded, tax free damages. It's a pisser but that's the way it goes, so I have reluctantly acquiesced to the request to leave out his real name. The least taxing substitute I can think of is asshole, so that's what it'll have to be.

"Can't hear you. Speak up. What's your name?" he asks once again.

Asshole mumbles his name once again, this time somewhat more audibly.

"Have you any identification on you?"

Asshole produces his wallet and removes his UCD student card, which he reluctantly hands to the cop, who examines it briefly.

"What are you studying in UCD, asshole?" (The cop obviously didn't say asshole, but I have inserted it in order to retain the natural flow of the exchange that took place.)

"Commerce and law," he says.

I couldn't help giving a contemptuous snigger. Little shit studying commerce and law and couldn't appreciate that the fundamental basis of commerce is the exchange of goods and services for legal tender, and that failure to remit same legal tender constitutes an infraction of contract law. Ironic really when you break it down, isn't it?

"Right asshole, listen to me now and listen good. This man brought you home and you refused to pay him. Are you aware that refusal to pay a legitimate taxi fare is an offence?"

"I haven't got any money ..."

"That's not what I'm asking you. Are you aware that failure to pay your taxi fare is an offence?"

"Yeah, I know, but ..."

"No buts, it's a serious offence and this man is quite within his rights to have you prosecuted. Do you know if you got arrested you'd never get a visa for the US or Australia and that any future employer could check to see if you had ever been arrested? Your commerce and law degree wouldn't be much use to you then, would it?"

After a minute or so, the potential ramifications sink in with asshole.They had sunk in with me about a minute earlier, and I was momentarily relishing the prospect of seeing this moron locked up for the night, successfully prosecuted and subsequently denied a visa of any sort, be it a work visa to go and do sod all in the affiliate office of daddy's firm or a holiday visa to go to the rugby world cup with the lads in Sydney.

"Look, I'm really sorry, okay? Finished my exams today and went on the piss with the lads. I'm really drunk, and I've no money to pay for the taxi. I'll bring it down tomorrow to you, I swear ..."

"No you won't," the cop says. "The state you're in right now, I'll be surprised if you get out of bed at all tomorrow. I'll tell you what we'll do. I'm off duty for a few days, so we'll say next Thursday, right? Six o'clock. In here. Right? You'll give this man his money and you'll apologise to him for wasting his time, okay asshole?"

"Yeah, okay, I will," he mumbles.

"Right, hang on there a second. I'm going to go and make a copy of this id and get your details."

The cop disappears in the back to do his thing. As soon as he's gone, asshole starts up with the snide looks and sneers again. I seriously wanted to deck him, but restrained myself.

"Right," the cop says, returning to the front desk, "what's your address?"

Asshole repeats the address he gave me initially and the cop writes it down in the incident book. He takes my particulars as well and confirms that I am agreeable to the solution he previously outlined.

"Yeah, alright," I said, somewhat disappointed I hadn't been able to hear the words "Book him Dano", knowing that a full body cavity search and a night in a cell lay ahead of him.

The cop gives us each a card with the details of the next rendezvous, warning asshole once more about the result of him failing to appear.

"Now asshole, I know you're drunk, but for your own sake, hear me good now. Six o'clock, next Thursday, in here with money and an apology. And if you're not here, I'll be up to your house to arrest you, you got that?"

"Yes, I'll be here," he says meekly.

"Right, on your way now. Go home, and I'll see you on Thursday. That okay with you?" he says to me, and I nod in agreement and thank him for his help.

As I walk down the steps to my car, moron is behind me. After looking around for a minute to get his bearings, do you know what he says to me?

"How'm I supposed to get home?"

Incredulous, I turn around and tell him to piss off and walk home. He slumps down on the steps and after a minute the cop comes out and tells him to clear off.

I go on my way but there's nothing much happening now, all the work's been mopped up and I'm still pissed off, so I head on home, hoping that asshole will lose the card and forget to appear the following Thursday.

No such luck though – Thursday rolls around and I arrive in

Blackrock police station at five to six to see asshole and his mother there before me.

I ignore them, go to the desk and ask for the cop who was dealing with the case. I'm told he's on his way back from his break and should be with us in a minute, so I stand on the other side of the lobby and wait for him. Asshole's mummy decides to intervene and approaches me cautiously.

"I am so sorry about this, really I am," she opens with.

"You've nothing to be sorry about, it's your asshole son who should be sorry," I interjected quickly.

"Well, yes, I know, and he will be, don't you worry. His father went beserk when he heard about this, said he'd disown him if anything like this ever happened again."

Sounded like a good idea to me. I said nothing, enjoying the way the situation made her feel uncomfortable.

"I'm sure you know how it is though when they finish exams and go out to celebrate ..."

"Oh I do yeah," I said. "I did exams every year for four years and got completely pissed after them all, but I still managed to pay for my taxi and get myself home without having to be dragged forcibly to the cops. Don't be making excuses for him. As far as I'm concerned, he's an arrogant little shit."

She was a bit taken aback at my response, but then the cop arrived out and ushered us into a little meeting room to put the matter to bed. Asshole and I take a seat at either side of a table, his mother and the cop choosing to stand.

The cop briefs the mother on the events of the previous week, and she starts shaking her head forlornly.

"That's not what he told me at all. He didn't arrive home until six in the morning, and his face was bleeding ..."

"His face was bleeding when he got into my car. I didn't do it, tempted as I was. I don't know what happened him after he left here, which was at about three am. The state he was in, it could well have taken him three hours to walk home."

"Look mum, just leave it, will you? I said that what I told you was a lie, okay?" poor little asshole said.

"No I won't leave it asshole. I want to know where you were until six o'clock in the morning and what you were doing to get yourself into that state!" she shouted, clipping round the back of the head, a measure which, if multiplied by a thousand and meted out at regular intervals over the preceding twenty-one years, might have staved off such an unhappy incident. I had said my piece before in the lobby though, so I decided to keep that particular thought to myself.

"Right, well that's a discussion for later on," the cop said. "I want to clear up this matter now. Asshole, have you got this man's money?"

"Yeah, here you go," asshole says, sliding exactly €6.80 across the table to me. "I'm really sorry about what happened and I'm sorry, for wasting your time ..."

"Right, are you happy that that's the end of the matter?" the guard asks me.

"Yeah, fair enough," I replied, still wishing I could deck him as well for good luck.

"Fair enough, do you want to shake hands now and that's the end of the matter?"

Both of us were equally horrified at the suggestion, but silently co-operated. I stood up to leave and asshole's mother once again apologised for her son's behaviour. I thanked the cop for his time and help and left the police station, asshole and his mother following behind me. I could hear her giving out to him and was somewhat pacified when I heard her shouting, "No you will not. You're grounded for a month and that's final!"

At least that was one less asshole I'd have to deal with, even if only for a month.

Poles Apart

This was back when I lived out in Bray. I was down in the village, or the "town" as the locals mistakenly refer to it, one afternoon, doing my rounds to the banks, making the minimum payments on my various term loans and credit cards, staving off the bailiffs for another month in an effort to maintain a clean credit record.

I was just pulling out my parking space directly outside the front door of the AIB on Main Street when this one in a tracksuit bangs on the window looking for a lift. I didn't want to take her at all. The traffic in Bray does my head in – I don't know how they fit so many bloody cars into such a small wee village. But before I could say anything she had her arse parked in the front seat and was issuing directions to where I could collect her friend. Not her boyfriend she hastened to add, "he's just a friend, nuttin' goin' on 'tween us". I've no idea why she felt the need to clarify this point, but I soldiered on to our next stop. Through the lights and I pull in at the bus stop to allow her male friend to get in.

"Right," she says, taking control of the situation, "we haf te get down the clinic b'fore it closes. D'ye know where id is, yeah?"

"Haven't a clue," I said.

"D'ye not know the clinic bud, no?" her escort says with disbelief.

"No I don't," I repeated, trying my hardest not to feel inadequate.

"Are ye local, no?"

Why was he asking me questions and then answering them himself? Technically I was living in Bray, but never particularly took to the place, so I had no desire to be considered a local.

"No, I'm not. I came out from town and just dropped off in the main street there," I said, before wondering why I had bothered to make excuses for my lack of knowledge.

"Alright, fair 'nough, I'll show ye. Straight on over de bridge, an' hang a left, yeah?"

I proceed as instructed down the Lower Dargle Road, over no less than sixty-three ramps. As we go the pair resume their conversation, oblivious to my presence.

"Whad I was sayin' Jay, yeah, was dat if I don't ged in here before four o'clock, dey won't take me sample, yeah, an' den I won't get me phy an' I'll be in bits, d'ye know whad I mean? We can up te de gaf after yeah?"

"Yeah, dat's kool Serena, kool, yew get yerself sorted. Lash dat coke into ye now, so you'll be able te go," he says.

"I'm bleedin' burstin' anyways," Serena says. "What time is it now?"

"Twenty to four," I add helpfully, as I near the T-junction at the end of the road. "Which way do you want here?"

"Hang a right bud, and a den a left, yeah?" Jay says.

I do so and enter a small housing estate, where I am further directed to a small community health centre. I stop and Serena gets out and runs inside. Jay politely suggests that I move up a bit and get my turn in so we're ready for the off. I comply and park on the other side of the road, checking quickly to make sure the meter is ticking away.

"Is it alright if I smoke, yeah?" Jay asks, answering himself unknowingly.

"Yeah, smoke away," I reply. I wasn't actually smoking myself at this stage, but always let punters smoke if they asked. Anything for a quiet life.

"Sound, d'ye want one yerself, no?"

Should have been on stage this lad, wowing audiences with his clairvoyant powers.

"No thanks, you're alright," I said, keeping an eye on the door for Serena's return.

"She won't be long bud. Dere'll be fuck all in dere at this time. Dey'll be all down de seafront tryin' te sell deir phy."

(A few words for those of you not familiar with the ins and outs of the rehab clinics run by the health boards. If you're trying to get off heroin and go into a clinic, they'll put you on methadone – phy – as a substitute, once you go in every week and give clean urine samples. If your sample isn't clean, they know you've been using again and they'll cut you off. There are plenty of holes in the system though. If you are still using, you can bring someone else's urine in with you in an identical beaker and do a quick switch in the toilet. Or you could take the phy, water it down a bit and sell what you don't need to someone who wants it so they can get a bit of sleep.)

"Yeah, fair enough," I said, not too pushed at this stage. I hadn't intended to start working this early, but seeing as how I had, I figured I'd stick it out and go from here. Turned my mobile on in case the base was looking for me. (They were sound in there – they knew I lived in Bray and that I usually started about seven, but if they had anything booked in on the system for Bray or Dun Laoghaire for around tea time they'd give me a ring with the details. Suited us both – I got a handy start, and they got a job off the screen that none of the other lads would be willing to travel out for.)

A couple of minutes later, Serena materialises and hops back into the car.

"Dat's dat outa de way, deadly, we go back up te yours or mine Jay?" she asks.

"We'll go te yours, yeah? Have ye got antin' t'eat in, have ye?"

"Ah yeah, dere'd loads in. Me ma dun de shoppin' dis mornin'."

"Deadly. I'm bleedin' starvin' I am. How's yer ma anyways?" Jay inquires, flicking his cigarette out the window.

"She's alright, ye know? Poxy veins are at 'er again … she's great wit Kylie dough, I'd be fucked widout 'er."

"Dat's good, dat's good. Whad age is Kylie now?"

"Two and a half Jay, yewage an' all she is, talkin' an everytin', she's great," Serena says happily.

We were headed up in the direction of Oldcourt now, which was a pain in the arse as it meant either snailing back up through the poxy village or hitting the motorway and getting snarled up in the mile long tailback of traffic taking the Killarney Bridge exit. I went for the village option in case they thought I was trying to run up the meter by heading for the motorway.

"Bud I'm telling' ye, dat day was de wurst day o' me life Jay. I mean, can ye imagine it? Me sister gives me seventy pound te put the notice in de paper fer me da's anniversary, and wha' do I do? Go an' buy a bleedin' bag and stick it in me leg. Den me ma finds me in a heap on de floor, dead te de world with Kylie screamin' 'er head off … I mean, Jaysus, what was I doin'?"

"I know chicken, I know, but dat's all behind ye now, ye're doin' great."

"Yeah," Serena says enthusiastically, "an' I'll be off dat shite soon enough as well, please God."

I get on to the Vevay Road at last and shoot up the rest of the way, turning right on to the Boghall Road. Jay directs me into one of the estates, towards Serena's house; she's gone all quiet now and sits staring out the window. Sounded like she had a pretty close call with the heroin a while back, and what a way to do it – using money intended for an *in memoriam* notice in the paper for your dad's anniversary to buy a bag of smack. I pull up and Jay sorts out the fare, despite Serena's protestations.

"No way, I'm getting' it, d'ye hear me?" Jay says, "sure amn't I 'bout te go in an' eat ye out o' house an' home?"

"Don't be stewpid, ye tick!" Serena says laughing. "Tanks mister, alright?"

"Yeah, no problem, all the best," I said, returning her smile.

"Dere ye go bud, keep de change. Sound, yeah?" says Jay.

"Oh yeah, cheers man, bang on," I said to Jay, thanking him for his generous gratuity.

It's always the way, the people who can least afford to throw you a quid for yourself wouldn't think twice about it, and some tosser going up to Foxrock would have their hand out for their 10 pence change.

I was just coming out of the estate when the phone rang. As hoped for, it was the base controller, ringing to give me the details of an account job. Three pick ups – Shankill, Cabinteely and Foxrock – and then into The Shelbourne. Sweet or what? Nice job to get the evening going, against the traffic mostly, and I finish up on the green. I pulled in to scribble down the details and headed towards Shankill. I normally don't like these addresses with just a house name, especially on small back roads. They can be a nightmare to find because most of the time the name of the house was painted on a by now moss covered granite rock about twenty years ago and is both invisible and illegible. At least I had what seemed like good directions and a mobile number just in case. Didn't need them as it turned out – newly painted pillars with name emblazoned on both of them, brightly illuminated to boot.

Big black electronic gates, but it was pissing rain and I couldn't be arsed getting out of the car so I gave a quick ring on the mobile to announce my arrival. A somewhat startled female voice expressed her pleasant surprise at my early arrival and buzzed me in. I sweep down the gravel driveway – love the noise a car makes on gravel, especially if it's a new Range Rover SE – and pull up at the door of a lovely ivy-clad period Victorian house, to be greeted by six security lights and the barking of what I figured was a very, very large dog. The front door opened and a glamorous woman in her early forties waved out to me. I acknowledge her and swing around, ready for the off.

A few minutes later, in she gets and once more remarks on how early I was. I explain that I lived in Bray and the base rang me, blah blah blah. Pleasantries thus exchanged, we get down to business and I proceed to Cabinteely for pick up number two. I have to say she was very friendly and down to earth, not at all snobby the way a lot of very wealthy people can be, mistakenly assuming that a massive bank balance somehow elevates them from the rest of the world.

I cruise down Cherrywood Road, under the old aqueduct and back out onto the dualler, and arrive a couple of minutes later at a new-ish development of mock-Tudor homes. Glamorous woman number two hops in and I head off to Torquay Road in Foxrock to collect number three, the wife of their host for the evening.

My three charges safely ensconced in the modest confines of my Jap import Corolla, I make tracks for The Shelbourne, gleefully whipping down the bus lane all the way into Donnybrook.

Conversation turned first to golf. One of the ladies was in a delicate situation – should she renew her membership in The K Club or Mount Juliet? Or continue with both? A tricky one this, but the girls methodically debated the pros and cons of both venues, covering crucial areas such as restaurant facilities, travel time, fellow members, availability of lessons from the resident professional, before eventually settling on Mount Juliet on the grounds that having a house on the grounds was really handy for long weekends.

Next on the agenda, seeing as how it was the first week of November, was what to wear for the legion of Christmas parties they were obliged to attend, and where to buy it. A simple black number won the day, but they were divided on where to buy the outfit itself. Arguments were heard in favour of a wide variety of stores like Kalu, Diffusion, Pia Bang, Marian Gale and of course, that old staple BT's.

Then arose the thorny issue of what to do for New Year's Eve. Now this was a tricky one for one of the ladies in particular who had to choose between catching up with the gang in Sandy Lane, or accepting an invitation to join some friends in the Burj A1 Arab hotel in Dubai for the festivities. Personally, I would have gone for Dubai, just to see the hotel, it looks like an amazing building, and anyway, Sandy Lane is *so* nineties really, isn't it?

Ah no, I'm being mean now, but seriously this was the conversation in the car on a wet mid-week evening in November heading into The Shelbourne. And there was nothing wrong with it *per se*, such were the circles these ladies and their friends moved in. I'm sure they and their spouses worked very hard in their respective jobs, and had been fortunate enough to enjoy a fabulous lifestyle, and fair play to them, you can't take it with you. It's just that it was such a contrast to the conversation I had overheard between Jay and Serena in Bray about an hour earlier.

Four or five miles apart, and yet worlds removed from each other.

I pull up outside the hotel and present my passenger with the account book for her to sign. It was a healthy enough fare what with the three pick ups, waiting time and distance travelled, and fair play to her, she added on a tip, but not without doing some mental arithmetic first I have to say. And for the record, Jay's gratuity worked out as a significantly higher percentage.

Soiling Charges

A lot of you may not be familiar with a fairly recent change in the fee structure that applies to public service vehicles. Next time you're in a taxi, peruse, as you are entitled to, the fare card on the dashboard. It lists the applicable extra charges that can be made during any given journey. Beside each one is displayed the amount of the charge and brief details of when they are applicable. On the reverse of the fare card, are some additional details. A "soiling charge" was introduced a while back, but the Office of the Director of Traffic in Dublin City Council decided, in deference to the sensitivities of the good people of the Dublin Taximeter Area, to refrain from describing the precise circumstances under which such a charge is payable. Personally, I wish they had, though thinking about it now, it would probably would have been of limited use, as those persons who commit such heinous acts would probably not be in a position to read the small print involved.

Now I like to think that I'm a pretty easy-going chap, and that I accommodate the requests of my punters in an obliging fashion, as the contents of this well written and handsomely presented tome no doubt illustrate. I'll gladly give a hooker a free ride home if she's had a crap night. I'll let teenage girls knock back the remains of their naggin of Huzzar before they get to Wesley. I'll be the soul of discretion when two horny devils let their lusty desires get the better of them and go at it like stray dogs in the back of my car. I'll run the risk of arrest for complicity so a strung-out junkie can score some gear down in Fatima Mansions. I'll let some fat, beer-stained rugby jock devour his kebab on the way home in the vain hope that it will absorb the sixteen pints he consumed in quick succession with the lads in Murray's after the match. I'll assist as best I can in the securing of the services of an escort for a visiting executive who doesn't want to waste the facilities that a generous expense account allowance affords him. But I will not, and I don't think I'm being unreasonable here, I will *not* allow some asshole to puke or piss in the confines of my car.

And it happens, people, it happens. More than you might like to think, especially the latter. And, it has to be said, the "ladies" amongst you are far and away the worst offenders in this category. For the record, I've never had a bloke do it in my car. They have no problem telling you to stop the car whilst they relieve themselves against a wall or in someone's garden, and however unsightly, ignorant or loutish it may be appear to the more genteel members of society – who are an endangered species at this stage – I can tell you it's infinitely more preferable to the alternative. It's quite a common sight really. You can't drive back from Galway on a bank holiday weekend without passing half a dozen blokes urinating into a ditch somewhere between Moyvalley and Enfield as the tailback wreaks havoc with their bladders.

Women on the other hand – in so far as I can figure out without the benefit of their contribution on the subject because they would be in no fit state to enter into a lively and informative discourse on the matter given the level of their inebriation – somehow manage to validate to themselves that it's okay to relieve oneself in the warm and cosy confines of someone else's car.

How they arrive at this justification, like so much else of the female psyche, is something I have yet to figure out. Is it the absence of adequate loo paper, or the unfamiliar surroundings of a car as opposed to a brightly lit vanity unit that would aid the application of make up and thus trigger the bowels into action? Or maybe it's the absence of a queue, which ironically, one would think, would assist in the development of a satisfactory holding technique? Answers on a postcard please.

Anyway, I think an example will illustrate the cogency of my argument.

Middle of the week, nothing special, pretty quiet out and even though I was parked first on the green with the base, I was cruising around looking for a fare. Going down Dawson Street I got a bloke coming out of Café Insane who was going out to Milltown. Didn't bother blowing in to the base to tell them, figuring I'd be out there and back in before they were looking for me, so off I went whipping out through Ranelagh. Dropped off in the apartments by the bridge and was just heading back in when my number was called. I acknowledged that I was indeed still parked up on the green and took the details of the job. Tore back down through Ranelagh and headed for The Unicorn restaurant on Merrion Row to pick up my passenger who was going out to Cabinteely on account. Lovely stuff, a nice long hop. Some lads hate these long fares, believing that it takes them out of the mix, but I'm more of a one-in-the-hand type man myself, especially when there's not much happening.

I park in my designated spot right outside the restaurant and go in to announce my arrival, where I am told that my passenger will be with me in a few minutes. Typical, after me risking an on-the-spot speeding fine to get there at the appointed time, I then have to wait for her to finish her bloody coffee. Back out to the car and flick on the meter, the company's paying for it, not her, and they've loads of money.

A few minutes later, out she comes, absolutely twisted, tottering along in her heels, trying in vain to get her arm in the sleeve of her coat as she walks. On the third grab of the door handle, she makes contact and climbs in, in a very undignified fashion I have to say.

Already knowing the general destination, I take off for Leeson Street to cross the canal and head for the dualler. Not a word out of her until we get to Donnybrook. She's just flaked out in the back seat, head back, gob open, muttering faintly to herself. It was still only about ten o'clock as well. Either she couldn't hold her drink at all or she had been lashing into the vino since six o'clock. Either way she was going to pay for this night of excess in the morning. She perks up a little when we get out to Montrose, looking around cautiously to get her bearings before straightening herself up and fixing her hair.

"So, how are you?" she says, as if resuming a conversation.

"I'm grand thanks," I reply. "How was your dinner?"

"What? Oh, dinner was fine, fine … fine, yes. Departmental thing, you know? Keep the troops motivated and all that shit," she said somewhat bitterly.

"Food good in The Unicorn?" I ventured politely.

"Oh yeah, it's really good. We go there quite a bit for work stuff, you know? I wasn't that hungry really, just had a starter and a few glasses of wine," she said modestly.

"Yeah right," I said in a sarcastic tone, knowing it wouldn't be detected.

At this stage, as I went galloping past Galloping Green, I had no idea of the events that were about to unfold. My main concern was that she didn't puke in the car, hence the little bit of banter to establish her condition. Totally pissed, but seemed to be holding it together, and not far to go now. Get her home, get the docket signed, get her out of the car, not my problem after that.

Past Cornelscourt, I noticed she was squirming around a bit. Lowered my window to let in a bit of cold air to keep her awake, and then asked her whereabouts she lived.

She slurred the directions and I proceeded as directed, eventually turning into her estate. I produce the docket book for her to sign and as she returns it to me, she drops the pen on the floor and gives out a little giddy chuckle. I smile patiently and reach back to pick it up off the floor, and as I do so, I get a whiff of something and detect a distinct increase in the temperature in the back of the car. I say nothing and examine the docket. Her signature resembled something like the hieroglyphics discovered in the caves at Lascaux, so I ask her for her name and print it in the space provided – didn't want the company querying the docket when their statement was issued.

She begins to gather her things together, wincing slightly as she does so, and then suddenly the magnitude of what has happened begins to dawn on me. I was absolutely horrified. It had to be. What else could it be? How could she? Jesus, this was gross. I thought I'd pretty much seen it all but this was a first, and what an unlikely perpetrator. Some wino bum, fair enough, you might be expecting it and would be watching out for it, ready to take evasive action. But her? A college-educated, well paid, paper-pushing middle manager? Holy shit. But what to do? Confront her? "Excuse me, could you please confirm to me that you have indeed urinated in the back of my car before I go absolutely apeshit?" No, too direct, which is admittedly normally my favoured approach, but what if I was wrong? She'd sober up pretty quick and totally freak out with me, and there'd be major hassle from the company the next day arising from my scurrilous accusations. But I wasn't wrong, she had definitely soiled my car, and I wasn't gonna stand for it.

I held my fire as she opened the door. I had no choice really, as for the first time in an awful long time, I couldn't actually think of anything to say. She mumbled a thank you and a good night and managed to extricate herself from the car. Once the door was closed, I flicked on the interior light and whirled around to inspect the crime scene. Though the seat covers were black, I could definitely see a small wet patch, little puffs of steam rising slowly off it, like smoke signals a diminutive tribe of Native Americans might send to their neighbours in the next valley. This was unbelievable. I turned around and stared out the front window and there she was, sashaying drunkenly up the driveway, aimlessly rooting in her purse for her keys.

Before she left the field of the beam of my headlights, I recognised a similar wet patch on the back of her skirt, one which I was sure the boys in the lab could match with that which was now slowly immersing itself in the foam of my back seat. I watched her fumbling at the front door, eventually gaining access and flicking on the hall light. A few minutes later, after negotiating a successful ascent of the stairs, a light in the upstairs bedroom goes on. I wait patiently for the light to go out, and quickly checking that the evidence was still clearly visible, I got out of the car and approached the door. Bracing myself, I rang the bell, deploying my signature technique of constant depression. Sure enough, within thirty seconds, an irate male roused from his slumber flung the door open.

"What the bloody hell do you think you're doing?" he bellowed at me.

"Good evening. Sorry to disturb you like this, but I have just brought your wife home from town. You may have gathered she is rather drunk, but what you may not have gathered is that she urinated in the back of my car and ..."

"What? What are you talking about?"

"Your wife relieved herself in the back seat of my car. You're welcome to inspect the damage if you wish," I said, gesturing back towards the crime scene, which I had sealed off in an appropriate fashion.

"Are you seriously telling me that you think my wife ... peed on the back seat of your taxi?" he asked in disbelief.

"I'm afraid so, and there is a soiling charge payable for such an offence. It's disgusting really, and I'm the one who has to go and clean the bloody thing up back at the base which means I'm gonna be off the road for a couple of hours," I explained.

He just stood there at the door for a moment, unable or unwilling to take it in.

"Hang on a second," he said, "just wait there, and I'll sort this out."

He turned around and ran back up the stairs to verify the facts of the situation with his wife. I was stood on the doorstep, but I could clearly hear every word of the conversation that took place, such was the volume, though it was pretty one-sided.

"Ann! Ann, wake up! Wake up! There's a taxi driver downstairs who says you pissed in his fucking car! Ann, Jesus Christ, look at the state you're in!"

"What? What is it? What's wrong?"

"I'll tell you what's wrong. You're fucking twisted, that's what's wrong! Did you piss in that man's car? Wake up! Jesus!"

"What? No ... I didn't. What's he saying?"

At this point the chap, realising he wasn't going to get a coherent answer from her, obviously inspected her clothes and found the incriminating damp skirt.

"Oh, for fuck's sake! I don't believe it! You stupid cow! How could you do something like that? Jesus Christ!"

Bingo! I felt utterly and totally vindicated. The broad dun it. Ann, however, still remained an un-cooperative suspect.

"What is it? I don't, know ..."

"That is so gross! Get up! Get up and go down stairs and apologise to that man. You're after ruining his car and now you're wasting his time! Get up!"

"No, I'm tired ... I don't want to ..."

"I don't care what you want. Get up ... Ann, Ann! Wake up! Jesus!"

She must have been totally wasted and had fallen back asleep. Next thing, a little girl appeared at the top of the stairs in her nightie, obviously woken up by the shouting.

"Daddy, daddy, what's going on? Why are you shouting at mummy?" she said.

Daddy appeared at the top of the stairs and tried to coax the little girl back into her room.

"Oh Jesus, go back to bed, darling. Mummy's had too much to drink, that's all, go back to sleep now, okay?" he said gently.

"Who's that man?" she said, looking curiously at me.

"Nobody, darling. Go back to bed, come on now."

Nobody. Thanks very much. I let out one of my trademark sighs and waited for daddy's return.

"Hello? Excuse me, I haven't got all night to be waiting around, you know?" I called up the stairs.

Daddy returns to the hall, suitably embarrassed by his now-comatose wife's antics.

"Right, I'm sorry, Jesus, she's, passed out up there. Ahm, what's the, how do we sort this out?" he said sheepishly.

"There's a standard fine of £20 payable in situations such as these. It's nowhere near enough in my opinion, should be more like a hundred. I have to go back to the base now and clean that up, gonna be off the road for a couple of hours, it's total bullshit, people getting themselves into that kind of mess. If I had my way, she'd clean it up herself. I'm not a nurse cleaning up after incontinent geriatrics ..."

"Yes, yes I agree with you, it's disgusting. I am so sorry, but there's nothing I can do with her at the moment, she's in no state to do anything about it. How much did you say it was? £20?"

"That's right," I said reluctantly.

"Right, give me one minute. I'll just get my wallet," he said, turning around to go up stairs again.

"Yeah, that's right Ann, you just sleep there while I take care of your mess," his voice drifted down from the bedroom.

He returned with his wallet and produced a single ten-pound note.

"Oh shit, I don't believe this, I've only got a tenner ..."

"I can add it to the fare on the docket if you like, but I'd have to put a note with it ..." I said, deviously willing to forego receipt of cash on the spot knowing the grilling she would face at work when the sordid details of the surcharge were explained to the account administrator.

"No, no, Jesus no, I work there as well. I'll deal with her in the morning, don't you worry. Hang on, I'll get some money from her purse," he said, turning around to bound up the stairs yet again.

Dead right too, she who pees is she who pays. He returns a minute later, wife's purse in hand.

"Now, here we are, let's see. There, there's £40, that's all there is, if there was more I'd give it to you, believe me, I know what hassle this is for you. I am really sorry about this, she just can't hold her drink, doesn't know when to stop herself ..."

"Fair enough," I said, taking the money off him. "It's still bullshit though, do you know what I mean?"

"Yes, yes I do. I am sorry," he said meekly.

I wasn't trying to have a go at him at all really. He was sound, and totally mortified at the behaviour of his wife, but it really is a complete pain in the arse when this sort of thing happens.

We said our goodbyes and he closed the door. I returned to my still idling car, got in and reversed out of the driveway. As I sped back down the dualler towards the base, I rolled down the windows to get some fresh air in the car to quell the stink of urine. I then called in to the base and told them to tell Robbie across in the car park to get the bucket and fairy liquid ready.

P.S. Difficult and all as it is to fathom, the grotesquery of the above story was topped during Christmas of last year. Not by events that took place in my car, thank God, but by a story a very good friend of mine told me. And I know it's true, as the culprit was sitting across from me at the time of its telling, head bowed in hands, cringing as the details emerged. (I won't name the young woman involved, but suffice to say that, being an asshole, I have but a handful of friends, and only a fingerful of them are married, and this woman is the wife of one of them – maybe two of them. I don't know for sure if polygamy's her thing or not.) Anyway, the topic of conversation had somehow turned to the rather unpleasant subject of people puking and peeing in taxis. I related the above tale, fully expecting my hosts and assembled friends to be suitably horrified, but as soon as I was finished the story, my pal starts shaking his head and told me he had an "even better" one, as he kind of proudly put it. Pointing a finger towards his lovely wife, he proceeded to recount the details of the night she found herself at the taxi rank on Dame Street the previous Christmas after attending a party and getting extremely drunk. Alone, and freezing cold in a little strappy dress, she was nearing the front of the queue when she was suddenly struck by an overwhelming desire to relieve herself. But what to do? She didn't want to leave the rank after queuing for so long, and even if she did, where would she go? It was about four in the morning and everywhere was closed, and she just wanted to get home. So do you know what she did? She just went. Right there and then, on the rank. Standing up. Thinking nobody would notice because they were all as drunk as she was. When she was all done, she shuffled around a bit and fixed herself as best she could, checking to see if anyone was giving her funny looks as hot steam rose from the pavement beneath her. As she turned around to have a look behind her, her eyes were met with the disgusted stare of what appeared to be a Frenchman, rooted to the spot with indignation and disgust at what he had just been witness to. Thankfully, a taxi pulled up a minute later and in she got, befouled and reeking, not a bother on her, and off home!

The Menagerie

This one was a freak, a complete and utter freak, and it was totally my own fault that I ended up with her in the car. But she'll never be in it again, believe me. The surreal, Dali-esque events of this particular night are forever seared on my consciousness.

It was unusually busy for a Thursday night and I had been on the go non-stop for a good eight or nine hours. I was coming down Harcourt Street but didn't like the look of any of the stragglers who were outside Copper Face Jack's looking for a taxi, so I headed on down to the green, where there was still a queue of about twenty people at the rank.

(I say at the rank, but they were in fact about half way up the rank side of the green. This often happens on a busy night. Instead of moving closer to the start of the rank as each person eventually gets a taxi, at some point the person next in line for a car decides they are not going to move down anymore and so the queue starts in the middle of the rank. But then what happens is, you get some moron who comes up Grafton Street and stands at the very top of the rank, conveniently ignoring the other poor sods thirty yards away, believing that by doing so they are entitled to get into the first car that comes along. What's even scarier is that successive morons silently agree with the strategy adopted by this particular moron and stand behind him, also ignoring the other poor sods thirty yards away. And so you have the legitimate queue standing in the middle of the rank, and the breakaway separatists declaring themselves a republic at the start of the rank. Inevitably some taxis will go to the start of the rank, believing those standing there are indeed next in the queue, thus, quite rightfully, incurring the wrath of those in the real queue, and some taxis will stop in the middle of the rank, thus, quite wrongly, incurring the wrath of the insurgents at the start of the queue. Confusing isn't it? This is also one of the main reasons fights start at taxi ranks, because sooner or later, these two queues merge and all hell breaks loose when some right thinking citizen who tries to mediate and explain to the contras that they should go to the back of the line ends up getting a smack from some drunken gouger who can't grasp the fundamental workings of an orderly queue. This is why I, and a good number of my comrades, choose to avoid ranks altogether and pick up along the streets as we head back into town, however inconsiderate this may seem to Joe Public. The message here is: don't wait at a rank, walk towards your destination and get a taxi on the way. It will get you home quicker, it'll work out cheaper and you'll have walked off a few hundred of your beer-ingested calories.)

So I pull up at what looked like the start of the legitimate queue, and the usual jostling ensues. This scruffy creature in a yellow oilskin raincoat marches purposefully towards my car, a small collapsible luggage carrier in tow, which had been haphazardly customised to increase its load capacity with the addition of the top part of a supermarket trolley tray, secured in place with a number of brightly coloured bungee straps. Some chancer opens the door and attempts to make a quick getaway, but she's having none of it.

"No, excuse me, I am next in line. I say," she says to me in a terribly posh and altogether jarring voice, "I am next in line, I am going out to Mulhuddart and I have money, here look, I can pay you in advance if you wish," she continued, rummaging in her pockets to produce a filthy twenty euro note, correctly presuming that I may have thought that, by her dishevelled appearance, she would not have the funds necessary to undertake such a journey.

"Wood ye go 'way oud o' dat, ye looper!" shouted the bloke who had tried to jump the queue. "Fly home on yer broom, bleedin' state o' ye!"

At this point, I reluctantly got out of the car to quell the looming fracas. The chap who I figured was indeed the rightful occupant of my car, and an altogether more preferable one at that, smiled politely and shrugged his shoulders.

"Well, yes," he said ruefully, "she has been here for some time jabbering on about getting home at this late hour. She was certainly here before him at any rate."

"Fuck yew, fat face, I'm takin' dis bleedin' car, right?" the scumbag continued in defiance.

"Look, I'm not sure who was first, but it definitely wasn't you and I'm not taking you anyway," I said to the inebriated moron, closing the back door before he could pour himself into the car.

"Yis are all wankers, d'ye know dat? Fuck de lod o' yis!" he said angrily, before eventually moving towards the back of the queue to no doubt harass whomsoever dared look sideways at him.

Another one or two people piped up that the old woman was next in line, so there was nothing for it but to open the boot and get her contraption inside and be on my way.

"You can put that in yourself," I said to her curtly. "I'm not touching it."

"That's quite alright, it folds down perfectly well," she replied instantly. "Here is my money, I am going out to Mulhuddart ..."

"Yeah, well, it might be more than that. Is that all you've got?" I said, looking for a possible out.

"It won't be more than that. I have taken taxis home before and that's more than enough," she replied indignantly.

I closed the boot with a heavy sigh and got back in the car, only to be joined in the front by herself. I had got a whiff of something unpleasant from her person as soon as I had got out, and now that we were in the confines of the car, it was magnified horrifically. I quickly opened both front windows and took off for Mulhuddart, determined to utilise the full capabilities of my 2.3 litre Volvo engine and set a new land speed record for the journey. We hadn't got to the end of Dawson Street when she started up.

"You must stop at a shop for me along the way. I have to get some provisions."

"I'm not stopping anywhere. You said Mulhddart, and that's where we're going. If you want to go shopping you can get out and get another taxi, right?"

"But there are one or two things I have to get," she said earnestly, expelling her whiskey breath right in my face which, coupled with the stench of her pungent body odour, almost had me puke in my own car.

I pulled in on Nassau Street at Judge Roy Beans and pointed in the direction of the Spar shop.

"There's a shop. You can get out here if you like, but I'm not waiting for you. Now make up your mind, okay?"

"Very well, drive on so. I have to get home to my animals, though I must say, it's very unreasonable of you," she says.

Home to her animals, I ask you. At this stage I had correctly sussed that this woman was a total loon, oblivious to the workings of the modern world, and that I could say just about anything I wanted to her and she wouldn't take it in at all. Sometimes when I have a complete nutter in the car, I just say nothing, get to my destination as quickly as possible, and get rid of them, but tonight I wasn't in the best of form for one reason or another, and wasn't at all in the mood for her own particular brand of shit.

"Is it now? Well, pity about you. You said Mulhuddart, and that's where we're going, directly. I haven't got time to be waiting for you to be doing your shopping. You could have done it before you went off drinking, couldn't you?"

"Excuse me, but I don't drink!" she retorted.

She didn't drink. Yeah, neither did Oliver Reed. Get a grip, woman. Rattled down over the cobbles on Eustace Street and out on to the quays, heading for the park.

"Where are you going? Where are you going? You should have gone up through Phibsboro, along the Navan Road to Blanchardstown and I would have showed you where to go!"

Tempted as I was to pull in and tell her where to go, I pressed on.

"Look, this is the quickest way to Mulhuddart at this time of night. There's about fifteen sets of lights the other way, there's none this way, okay? Now just shut up, will you?"

My head was wrecked and we weren't even in the park yet.

"You're a very cross young man if you don't mind me saying so …"

"No, I don't mind at all."

"Are you always like this? It's not a very positive way to live your life, would you not agree?"

Jesus, that's all I needed. Pop psychology from a drunken, smelly, oilskin-clad, tree-hugging, animal-loving septuagenarian at three in the morning.

"Look I've had a long night, and I don't need this shit from you, alright? Just leave it, okay?"

At last she shut up, and I lit a badly needed cigarette.

"You shouldn't be smoking, it's very bad for you! And you certainly shouldn't be smoking whilst driving a taxi! Have some consideration for your passengers!"

Now, technically, she was correct to a certain degree. Smoking is very bad for you, but it was my taxi and if I wanted to smoke, I was going to smoke. If a punter asks if they can smoke, I will always oblige if it means keeping them quiet, because as far as I'm concerned, a quiet punter is a good punter. Me, I can normally hang on until someone is out of the car and then enjoy my smoke in peace on the way back into town or wherever. But she was stressing me out, and I didn't feel obliged to ask her if she minded if I smoked.

Though I was avoiding eye contact with her, I could see out of the corner of my eye that she was staring intently at me. And then do you know what she says to me?

"May I have a cigarette?"

"What? You're just after telling me how bad they are for me and how inconsiderate I am, and now you want one? No, you can't have one. Jesus, are you on drugs or what?"

"No, I am not on drugs. How dare you suggest something like that? I smoked for a good number of years, and occasionally get a craving for one myself, that's all! May I have one?"

"No, you may not, okay?"

I'd normally happily give a passenger a cigarette as they got out of the car if they had run out and wanted one last smoke before they went to bed, but not this looper, no way.

Another minute's blissful silence elapsed as I passed the monument in the park beside the Aras. It was quite foggy out and I flicked on my full beams to check out the road ahead. Then she grabs my arm and shrieks, "Slow down, you'll hit the deer! You'll hit the deer! They're the most beautiful animals! So graceful, be careful!"

"Look, leave the driving to me, okay?" I snapped back at her, no more than a split second before Dasher, Prancer, Rudolph *et al* leapt across the road in front of me.

"Oh my God, you nearly killed them all!" she shrieked, "You could be fined for that."

My head was totally wrecked at this stage, so I said nothing and tore along, through the gates, straight through Castleknock village, across the flyover at the shopping centre. Nearly there, thank God. Nutter then tells me to turn down this narrow road, once again advising me to slow down, as "people walk down here all the time, night and day".

"Stop! Now, there's my house, see. And all my little darlings! Yes, I'm home! Look how excited they are!"

Okay. First, "house" was a gross exaggeration. I've seen cardboard boxes bear closer resemblance to a house. Her home was in fact a glorified lean-to, looking for all the world like something little kids would make in the space of an hour whilst playing in the forest for a day during the summer. And second, the "little darlings" she referred to were all manner of farmyard animals. Whilst not wishing to hang around and do a complete inventory, I definitely spotted two goats, at least one pig, about half a dozen chickens, any number of cats and dogs, and a bloody horse. No deer though, now that I think about it. A make-shift fence enclosed the dirty, shit-ridden yard right beside her "house".

I totalled the meter and she again produces the filthy twenty-euro note.

"That's not enough," I said, pointing at the meter, which read about twenty-three something.

"Well, it's always been enough before. There must be

something wrong with that thing," she replied, gesturing disdainfully at my recently installed and calibrated meter.

Sod it, I thought. I wasn't going to get anywhere with this fruitcake. Better to cut my losses and get the hell out of this armpit of the universe.

"Jesus. Right, come on, get out of the car," I capitulated.

I got out and opened the boot to yank out her trolley contraption, dropping it unceremoniously on the ground. She was taking ages to get out, and I had to go over and open the door to coax her. Despite my desire to get away as quickly as possible, there was no way I was touching any part of her apparel to assist her.

"Come on, will you, I haven't got all bloody night," I barked impatiently.

"Yes, yes, I'm coming. My word, you really are an impatient young man," she said, finally upright.

I slammed the door shut and went around to my side and hopped in, engaging reverse before the door had closed, nearly knocking her over in the process as she bent down to reassemble her cart. I tore back down the road, ignoring the damage the rough surface would do to the undercarriage of my car – I just wanted out of there.

It was pretty cold out, but I had all four windows down as I sped back along the Blanchardstown bypass, breathing through my mouth as much as I could. Making a mental note to stop in Spar in Phibsboro to buy fourteen air fresheners, I reached for my cigarettes. They weren't on the dash where I had left them. I looked on the floor and around my seat, thinking that I had maybe brushed them to the ground in my haste to get out of the car. No sign of them anywhere. Then I remembered that as I opened the side door to hurry her along, she looked a bit suspicious. Smelly old cow had robbed my smokes!

Lock up your daughters

Wesley in Donnybrook on a Friday night is quite a phenomenon really. Every Friday evening, all over the southside of Dublin, teenagers spin a meticulously fabricated web of lies to their parents as to their supposed whereabouts and movements for the night ahead. Victoria tells her "mom" that she's babysitting with Rebecca. Rebecca tells her "mom" she's babysitting with Victoria. Victoria and Rebecca both leave their house at the appointed time, appropriately dressed in combats and sweat tops. They meet up and go to a third party's house, whose parents thankfully exercise less parental control than their own. There, with the assistance of fake tan, glitter and more make up than is usually available at the Max Factor concession in Brown Thomas, they transform themselves from innocent fifth year students into sophisticated Lady Victoria Hervey wannabes, resplendent in little black dresses and heels.

After sneaking out of the house unnoticed, they assemble with other like-minded teenagers, and lots of boys, to consume copious amounts of alcohol, vodka being the drink of choice, because it leaves the least trace of alcohol on their breath. With the alcohol in their system helping to act as a social lubricant, it is not uncommon at this point for the young girls to pair off with their platonic male friends to practise their sexual techniques, lest they be subject of unkind taunts about their lack of sexual prowess from their conquests later on in the evening. Suitably rehearsed, the groups converge in Donnybrook, most opting for the forecourt of the Shell garage and the surrounding premises to join up with each other. This is a critical time, as it is used by all present to scout out suitable prospects of the opposite sex whom one may wish to make a play for later on in the disco. Girls would be quizzing each other to assess where a particular guy might go to school, where he lives, if he plays rugby, and crucially, if he has access to a car. Guys would try to find out from their own network about who a particular girl may have gone out with before and how far that chap had been able to get with her.

Then comes the hard part – getting in to Wesley itself in order to move things forward. Identification is obviously critical here. If you happen to be eighteen, obviously a passport will suffice. But by the time you've reached eighteen, unless your social development leaves an awful lot to be desired, you should have moved onwards and upwards to the rarefied pastures of regular pubs, from where you can now gleefully sneer at the children who have taken the place you occupied only one short year ago. If you're under eighteen, however, you need a good fake id in order to gain access to the pleasure palace. Gone are the days when you could get some dodgy id laminated in the local video shop. Now you need the real thing. This is where your friend's older brother in UCD comes in to play. For a modest one-off fee, he can procure stolen blank student union ids, onto which the appropriate details and photograph can be placed. Now, not only must you be able to walk the walk, you must be able to talk the talk. Hence the frantic last minute memorisation of false dates of birth, which are in themselves a rite of passage for today's teenagers. Get it wrong, and you skulk around outside for a couple of hours in the freezing cold. But get it right, and yours are the keys to the kingdom of heaven.

And so the chosen few hundred gain access and have their hopes and dreams for the evening shat upon by their best friend, who snogs their intended conquest, while the pathetic losers outside have to contend with whatever lewd acts of public indecency they can get away with without attracting the attention of the odd passing squad car or cops on the beat, who more than likely are too busy talking on their mobile phones to notice anything out of the ordinary.

And so the glitter ball stops revolving after the last slow set, and the hordes of lusty teenagers spill out on to the roadside. This is when things can get really interesting. It wouldn't be a Friday night at Wesley without a running street battle between two or more gangs of lads, eager to display their primal qualities and kick the living shit out of each other in the hope of impressing the fairer sex with their strength. Or seeing some girl puking her ring up at the bus stop, while yet another little princess is consoled by her friends as her new boyfriend of two hours ago snogs some other girl across the road.

And so it was one Friday night as I cruised down past Montrose heading back into town. I had been working since about five and was already getting tired, even though it was just about midnight. As I passed the Shell garage a young girl in an outrageously short skirt flagged me down. I pulled in and she beckoned to her friends to join her. In they get, four stick thin pageant queens in regulation issue black outfits. Let's call them Emma, Victoria, Melanie and Geri.

"Okay, where're we going first?" says the blond in the front, taking control of the situation.

"Emma's first," said one of them.

"Yeah, but she can't go home like that, her mom will kill her," explained blondie.

"Her clothes are at my house, but we better hurry, my parents will be home soon."

"Okay, Goatstown please."

"Yeah, no problem," I said, and cut through the petrol station to get back out on to Eglinton Road.

"Emma? You okay?" asked one of the girls in the back, leaning across to check on her friend. "Jesus, she's like, totally fucked."

I checked out the back seat to see which one was Emma, and what constituted being "totally fucked" these days. She didn't look too hot alright – hair in a mess, eyes streaming, make up all over the place.

"I bet it was that sleazy bastard Ryaner that did it," said the other one as she fixed Emma's hair and rubbed her arm.

"No way, he's really nice, I was with him earlier on," said blondie in shock, whirling around to confront the one who would dare impugn the integrity of her new beau.

"You were with loads of guys, Victoria. That doesn't make them nice," hissed the accuser cattily.

"Fuck you, Melanie, just because you didn't score," Victoria retorted.

With friends like these, huh? I was cracking up to myself at all this. God, I'd feel sorry for young people these days if they weren't such insecure morons.

"Emma, you okay?" asked Melanie. "We're nearly home."

"Don't feel well, think I'm gonna be sick," Emma eventually said, much to my dismay.

"Maybe she just drank too much, you don't know he spiked her drink ..." Victoria protested further.

"He did, the wanker, he was sleazing around her all night. I'm gonna ring Collie tomorrow and ask him ..." said Melanie.

"Oh yeah, like he's gonna tell you his best mate slipped something in her drink! Get real Melanie, Jesus," sighed Victoria, flipping down the sun visor to check herself out in the mirror.

"Collie will, he's sound. He wouldn't have anything to do with that kind of shit. Ryaner's a bastard, he really is," Melanie continued.

I turned right into the estate and was directed to what turned out to be Melanie's house. I pulled in at the gate and Melanie got out and turned around to help Emma.

"Have you any money, Emma?" Victoria said.

"What? Oh yeah, hang on a second ..."

"Jesus Christ Victoria, don't be such a cow, can't you see she feels like shit?" said the other girl in the back, who had been pretty quiet up until now.

"What's up with you?" scowled Victoria, whirling around. "I've only got five euro!"

"Fine, well I'll pay the rest," she said, before leaning over to close the open door. "Don't worry about it Emma, I'll get it. Text me tomorrow, yeah?"

"Yeah I will. Thanks Geri, bye," said Emma, managing a faint smile.

Two down, two to go.

"Where to now?" I said, as if everything was hunky dory.

"She's next," said Victoria dismissively.

"Ahm, I'm going to Kilmacud please."

"Yeah, no problem," I replied cheerily.

She was sound, as were the other two who had just got out. Don't know what they were doing hanging around with the bitch in the front of the car though. Thought she was the ultimate prom queen, and that other mere mortals would be delighted to move in her exalted circle. I suppose every class has at least one, and they normally land on their arse sooner or later. I turned right at the Spar, cutting through Rathmore to get out on to the Upper Kilmacud Road without going over any bloody ramps. Geri directed me to her house and when I pulled in, she took a tenner out of her purse and more or less flung it at Victoria.

"Fuck you Victoria, you're such an asshole, do you know that? Thank you."

"You're welcome, all the best," I said, smiling. You're right as well I said to myself.

"What*ever*," Victoria said as the door closed, "I'm going to Leopardstown."

I nodded and headed up through the industrial estate.

"So, did you have a good night?" I asked, trying to wind her up, ignoring the fact that the three girls she went out with a few hours earlier now thought she was a complete bitch.

"What do you think?" she replied haughtily.

"I don't know, I don't think your friend Emma had a great time, judging by state she was in."

"God, it was like her first time in there? And she only got in because she was with me. I know *all* the bouncers."

"Oh yeah? So what happened her? She looked like shit."

"I don't know, I wasn't with her for the whole night. I was talking to some girls from Alex, and then when I came back, Melanie's all dramatic, saying some guy spiked her drink and tried it on with her …"

"And is there much of that shit going on in there?"

"A bit. Guys'll try anything to score. But did you see the way Melanie just blamed that guy straight away? That's only because she thinks he's cute and he wouldn't go near her in a fit. He told me. She's so naïve."

"And how do you know it wasn't him?"

"Because I was with him most of the night. Anyway, I know who it was," she said dramatically as I turned right into her estate.

"Why didn't you say anything so?" I asked.

"It was Collie. And they all think he's so sweet. But it's just an act, he's a total scumbag. His older brother knows my brother and he's a dick as well, always sleazing around me when he's in our house."

Victoria sighed heavily as she put her change back in her purse.

"Thanks, g'night."

"All the best," I replied.

I watched her go in and turned the car around to head for Dun Laoghaire. And people think there's something wrong with me for not wanting kids? I don't think so.

Cops

I was driving down Thomas Street one night during the week in late February of last year, heading back from Inchicore. It was about one in the morning and this part of town was practically deserted. The lights at the Meath Street junction changed and I reluctantly hit the brakes. It was a fairly mild evening and I had my window down, enjoying a cigarette, when next thing I hear a woman screaming across the road and whirl around to have a look at what's going on. And there, in the doorway of the old Irish Permanent on the corner of Meath Street and Thomas Street, there's this guy having a go at a woman he has penned in the doorframe. The lights had changed at this stage, so I got through the yellow box, parked up on the kerb outside the NCAD, and got out of the car.

Now, alcohol-induced rows are nothing new and don't really bother me in the slightest. I actually quite enjoy them some of the time, once they don't get too heavy. And most of the time they're over the stupidest thing in the world, like some bloke innocently checking out some girl's arse when he thinks his girlfriend is in the loo and she happens to be standing right behind him. Or *vice versa*, that kind of thing. Stupid, maybe, but nothing that significant in the grand scheme of things, and most of those involved always seem to get over it, with quite a number of them, my friend Sue included, actually thriving on the drama such events bring into their lives.

This was different though. This girl looked like she was being harassed or interfered with or something like that, and I couldn't just drive past her and pretend I hadn't seen it. So I run across the road to see if she's okay, and as I get near them I hear her shouting, "Stop it! Just stop it, please!" I shoved my way in between them and pulled the girl out from the doorway, telling her to go over to my taxi. Her drunken assailant turns to me and tells me to fuck off, shoving me backwards. The girl hesitates for a second and then starts to run down the road. Your man whirls around to me and before I know what's happened, he punches me and I'm on the ground. Now I'm no street fighter, and he was a big burly bastard, and I was totally shitting it, so when I got up, more than a little dazed, I headed for the relative safety of my car. He was twisted drunk and started stumbling down the road after the girl, so I tore down the road after her and told her to get in. Scumbag was on his way, shouting his head off, so she eventually gets in and I take off down towards Christchuch.

Not a word is spoken for a minute or so, until I swing a right at Burdock's and pull in. My jaw is killing me, tender and kind of numb at the same time, and I'm not with it at all. I light up a smoke, despite the pain involved in inhaling, and offer one to my passenger. She stops sniffling, and looks at the cigarette for a second, as if trying to remember if she smoked or not. She takes it and I light it for her.

"Thank you," she said softly.

"You're alright, I've got loads," I replied, trying to make a joke out of it.

"No, I mean, for ..." she said, cracking a faint smile.

"Yeah, I know what you mean. What the fuck was all that about? Do you want to go the cops?"

"No, no, I can't, I can't ..."

"What do you mean you can't? Some psycho's trying to smack the head off you. For fuck's sake, of course you can go to the cops. That's what they're there for ..."

She sucks on her cigarette and stares out the window for a minute before answering me.

"He's my boyfriend, and he is a cop ..."

Holy shit, she sure knew how to pick them.

"So what, just 'cos he's a cop doesn't mean he can give you a smack whenever he feels like it ..." I reasoned.

And then of course, came the classic response.

"He didn't mean it, he's only like this when he's drunk ..."

"Oh well that's grand then, isn't it? Here's me worried about you for no reason. Would you cop on? Is he gonna give up drinking then, and this'll never happen again, is that what you're saying?"

"What? No, I suppose not ..."

"Definitely not, once is once too much. You have to report him, okay? I'll go with you now if you like, and they'll have to do something about it ..."

"I did, once before, but he got it sorted out, and nothing ever happened ... he knows them all," she said sniffling.

She still wouldn't really make eye contact with me, like she was embarrassed or something. Your man must have been a complete asshole, totally possessive, a bit like that nutter Trevor in Eastenders.

"And what's gonna happen now? You're not going home, are you? Do you live with that moron?"

"Yeah, I do, but it'll be okay, he won't come home now after this. He'll go to his friend's house for the night. And then arrive up tomorrow with some flowers and say how sorry he is ..."

"Yeah, and everything's grand until the next time. Jesus, what are you doing this to yourself for? Leave him, or tell him to fuck off and get his own place. You don't need this shit, do you?"

She shook her head slowly.

"I don't know if I can, he won't leave it at that ..."

"How long are you going out with him?"

"Three years ..."

"Three years! Jesus, are you mad? Do you not get out much or what? I know most men are dicks, but surely you can do better than that asshole? What age are you?"

"I'm not telling you what age I am," she said smiling. "What age are you?"

"Thirty-two, going on fifty."

"You don't look thirty-two."

"I know yeah, that's the oil of ulay, you know? Worked for my mam, thought I'd give it a shot ..."

She was a bit more together now, more relaxed, and the hankies were gone.

"So what do you want to do? Do you want me to drive you round to the cop shop or what? I'll go in with you, say I saw him having a go at you ..."

"No, no, really. Thank you, I know you're only trying to help, but believe me it won't do any good, honestly. I'll just have to sort it out myself."

"Well at least stay with a friend or something tonight, don't go back there on your own ..."

"He won't come back. I know he won't. He never does when this happens. He sleeps it off in his friend's place and arrives home after his shift the next day, all full of apologies ..."

"Yeah, you said that, but wouldn't it be good if you weren't there when he got home with his poxy flowers and he thought you'd split? Might make him cop on a bit."

"I know ... yeah I might. I think I'll just go home first, though, okay?"

"You sure?"

"Yes, yes thanks."

"Fair enough. Whereabouts are you?"

"Off the South Circular, near Kelly's Corner."

"Right so," I said, taking off down Werburgh Street. I cruised through the lights at Kevin Street and on up Heytesbury Street to the lights at South Circular Road, which were definitely green as I went through them.

"Just here is fine, thanks. How much is that?"

With all the drama, I'd forgotten to put on the meter, but even still, as big an asshole as I am, I wasn't going to charge her for the ride home.

"Jesus, don't worry about it. I'll tell you what. I'll hang on here a minute, you grab a few things and I'll drop you over to a friend's house, yeah?" I said encouragingly.

She smiled once more as she fixed her hair and buttoned up her coat.

"No really, thanks, but I'll be fine, seriously," she said assuredly, nodding her head for emphasis, "and thank you for the lift, really, it's very good of you. Goodnight."

She leaned over and gave me a peck on the cheek before getting out of the car. I watched her climb the steps to her flat and waved as she closed the door. What else could I do? Jack shit, so I took off around by the canal to Portobello to look for a fare. And who knows what happened her? I never even got her name.

Passport Control

Sunday night and it was nice and lively, a good few punters out drinking, and not too many taxis out, which was nice, as the man says. Don't know what it is about Sunday nights, but there are loads of taxi drivers who just will not work it. Even if they've had a crap week, they won't go out for a couple of hours and get a few quid together. Now, after a long Friday and Saturday night, which you absolutely have to do if you're going to make anything at all, it is nice to chill and have a few beers on Sunday, but I'd rather do that on a Tuesday or Wednesday, when you know it's going to be dead on the streets.

It was about eleven and I was over on the northside, coming back from Donaghmede. Four lads hailed me down on Tonlegee Road. The Golden Mile, northside taxi lads call it, on account of how busy it is, but I've never really found it to be that way myself. I don't make a habit of touring around there that much. I'd sooner head back into town and park up somewhere with the base, but there you go, each to his own.

So I pull in and the lads pile in, three of them scrambling for the back door and shoving one lad towards the front.

"Ged in dere yew, ye miserable bastard, you're payin' fer dis and dat's fuckin' dat, righ?"

"Alright lads, where're we off to?" I ask.

"Ah, town please, bud, yeah?"

"Town it is," I say and bang on the meter.

"Bollix, we're not goin inte town, Deco. We're always in bleedin' town wit dem. Why don't we go somewhere else?" complained one of the lads.

"Alrigh, alrigh, well where so, moany arse?" Deco replied.

"We could go te Nite Owls," added the lad in the front helpfully.

"Who assed yew, Golly?" said Deco, slagging.

"Fuck off Deco or I'll bleedin' burst ye," Golly replied before turning around. "Look, when were we last out widout de quare ones? Bleedin' ages ago, so what's de point o' goin' inte town? We won't be able te have a laugh anywhere widout it gettin' back local, yeah? So we'll go te Nite Owls, bleedin' rapit id is ..."

"What the fuck is Nite Owls, an' where is it?" asked one of the other lads.

"Nite Owls! It's in Renelegh, ye bleedin' tick! D'ye not know antin'?" scorned Deco.

"Fuck yew Einstein, I'm just bleedin' askin' alrigh? Is id any good Golly?"

"Fuckin' deadly id is Del. A few o' de lads outa de job were dere dey udder week, said it was great."

"Fair 'nough, sounds good te me."

"Fuckin' Renelegh, where's dat? Up de bleedin' mountins is it?" asked the other lad.

"Jaysus super, Renelegh, on the soutside, ye know where id is ..." said Golly.

"De soutside! Ah goodnite, ask me bollix, I'm not goin' over dere. It's bleedin' miles away!" he protested.

"Fuck's sake, superman, it's onwney over de bleedin' canal. Would ye relax de kax, yeah?" said Derek.

"Superman?" I asked inquisitively.

"What? Oh yeah, well his name's Kent, ye know? Superman. Clark Kent, yeah? D'ye geddit?" Golly filled me in.

"Oh right, very good, very good. So wherc're we going now, Ranelagh is it?"

"Yeah, sound," said Golly, and then after a pause, "So are ye busy tonigh?"

The three lads cracked up laughing in the back at Golly's opening gambit.

"Are ye busy tonigh'! Ye muppet! How many bleedin' times a nite d'ye tink people ask 'im dat?" says Deco laughing.

"Jus' tryin' te make bleedin' conversation, fuck youse," replied Golly undaunted.

I was laughing to myself as well I have to say. People must ask me that about twenty times a night, quite often after they may have been waiting an hour or more for a bloody taxi, when I would have thought the answer was obvious.

"Ah yeah, ticking along nicely," I replied politely, as we headed through Fairview.

"Where're dey all goin' anyways?" asked Derek a minute later, nodding his head backwards, referring no doubt to the "quare ones" from whose watchful eye the lads had escaped for the night.

"Tamangos o' course, where else?" said Deco, "an' did ye see de state o' dem goin' off? Dressed up te de bleedin' nines dey were!"

"I know yeah, an' dey'll be givin' it lodes up dere an' all ..." added Golly.

"Yeah, an' if we were dere an' so much looked at some young one's arse dere'd be murder, lode o' me bollix, it really is ..."

complained Deco.

"Yes dere wood," agreed Golly solemnly.

"Hope dere's some tasty birds in here now," mused Deco optimistically.

"Oh yeah, an' lads, I know I don't need te say it, but what goes on tour, stays on tour, yeah?" said Derek.

"Relax Del, it's kool man, yeah? Mum's de word," reassured Deco. "Sure Tracey never sussed it about dat bird yew were wit a while back, didden she not?"

"Jaysus, dat was nuttin' man, sure I didn't even shag her!" protested Derek.

"Just as bleedin' well," said Superman. "She was owney about sixteen!"

"Yeah, she hadden even dun her poxy Leavin' hadden she not?" said Golly laughing.

"Nider have I, an' I'm twenty-bleedin'-seven!" laughed Derek. "An' yew slaggin' me?" he continued, "least I bleedin' scored, yew wudden get yer end away in a brottle, ye ugly sap! Just as well yer mot's blind, she'd run a fuckin' mile if she could see yer horrible bleedin' face!"

"Fuck yew Del," argued Golly, "yew didden ged antin' in Liverpool dat time we went over, an' we may as well 'ave bin in a bleedin' brottle wid all de brazzers dere gaggin' fer it!"

"Time out lads, time out," said Superman the mediator, "yis are boat ugly bastards, an' let's leave id at dat, yeah?"

"Oh, wud ye lissen to 'im," raged Golly, "de las' bid o' tit yew saw was yer bleedin ma's!"

"Nuttin' wrong wid dat, his auld one has a fine pair," said Deco. "Least she did de las' time I saw dem!"

"Ye scruffy bastard!" shouted Derek.

"Yew leave my auld one outa dis, ye pox!" shouted Superman, hitting Deco a dig on the shoulder.

At this point, we all creased up laughing. With sabre-like wit such as this, there would be no winner. We were stopped at the lights at College Green and a procession of foxy chicks crossed the road.

"Speakin' o' baps, wood ye look at the pair on yer one?" said Golly, rolling down his window, "Alrigh ladies, where're yis off te dis evenin' den?"

The girls in question smiled back at the lads, two of them giving a little shimmy for their entertainment.

"Go on yis good tings!" roared Superman out the window.

I pulled off and went down Nassau Street to head for the green.

"Town's hoppin' tonite innit?" commented Derek.

"Fuckin' sure id is, shud be a right lode up here now an' all," said Golly enthusiastically.

"D'yew have shares in dis kip or what?" asked Superman. "Why don't we ged out here an' see what's happenin'?"

"Nah fuck it, super, we'll go on out te Renelegh fer de crack, relax," said Derek. "May as well, God knows when we'll be on de tear again, d'ye know whad I mean?"

"Fair 'nough, bud if it's shite we're spilttin' back inte town, yeah?"

"Oh yeah, definite-ley. Whad are we drinkin' lads, pints or shorts?" asked Derek.

"Start wid a few pints anyways, yeah?" said Deco, "mite go on te de Red Bulls after dat."

"Sounds like a plan," agreed Golly.

"Bollix te dat, I'm not touchin' dat piss, man, fucks ye up it does," warned Superman.

"Ye bleedin' blouse, we'll get yew a Baileys den, alrigh' chicken?" said Deco.

"Fuck off, dat does me head in, dat stuff, I'll be hangin' in de morning, an' I'm on an early shift," reasoned Superman.

"Yeah, yeah, yer're nod able fer it, super, yer're geddin' old, dat's what de problim is," said Deco.

The lads got serious for a minute to discuss their story for the bouncers, agreeing on their provenance, in much the same way as Sotheby's or Christie's do when trying to legitimise the origins of an antiquity they knowingly purchased from an Italian *tombaroli* via his Swiss fence.

"... no, no we go in two be two, dat's de way, righ'? An' if dey ask is where we were before, we say we had a quick pint in Ratmines, yeah?" confirmed Golly.

"Why? Jus' say we were in town, fuck dem," argued Superman.

"Don't be a sap, super, jus' play it my way will ye, or ye won't bleedin' ged in, righ?" cautioned Golly.

"Cop on, super, we're goin' in here fer a good laugh, yeah? Now be kool," pleaded Derek.

"Righ'! Righ', relax will yis? Everyone got deir passports?" inquired Superman as I crossed the canal at Charlemont Bridge. "We're on de soutside now!"

"We were on de soutside when we crossed the Liffey, ye muppet!" corrected Deco.

"I know dat, ye fool, I mean de real soutside dough, de posh bit, yeah?"

"Here is kool bud, yeah?" requested Golly.

I stopped at the bus stop before the nightclub, flicked on the light and totalled the meter.

"Dey like te see ye walkin' up a bit so dey know yer're not buckled, d'ye know whad I mean?" he explained winking at me.

"Oh yeah, you have it sussed alright," I replied smiling.

The three lads pile out of the car quickly, leaving Golly to pay the fare.

"Scroungy bastards!" Golly calls after them. "Now, how much is that bud?"

I settle up with Golly and give him his change, but he shakes his head.

"Nah, nah, not a' tall bud, sound. Good luck, righ'?"

"Bang on man, cheers, all the best," I reply gratefully.

The boys march on up to the steps and after a comparatively brief interrogation, gain access to the now extinct Night Owls.

I hoped it would be worth the journey.

Do you know who my daddy is?

I was coming back from Carpenterstown one Thursday night, about one am. Not a whole lot of people out, especially out here. Always amazes me the amount of people who lived out there in Luttrellstown, Laurel Lodge, Roselawn and the like and yet I rarely got a fare into town with any of them. Then come a Friday or Saturday night and I could be up and down through the bloody park ten times bringing them home. In all my time driving a taxi, I could count on one hand the number of times I've got a return fare into town from the village as I dropped off out there. So I'm not likely to forget anything remotely interesting that happened on such a journey.

As I said, I had dropped in Carpenterstown and had successfully negotiated the forty-three roundabouts impeding my return to the familiar environs of the Castleknock Road – it's getting like bloody Lucan out there – when there it was, a fare for me. Gleefully hit the brakes at the petrol station opposite Myo's and in they get – two very good looking ladies, dressed to kill and out to party by the looks of them.

"Hi! We're going into Renard's, okay?"

"Yeah, cool," I said casually.

Sweet, nice long hop into town, get me back in the middle of things nicely.

"Yeah, we just have to stop off at my house for a second. I have to get some money."

"Whereabouts is it?"

"Straight on down past the Georgian Village. I'll show you where," one of them says to me, before continuing in earnest the conversation she had been having with her friend before they got in the car. They were fairly well on, the pair of them, really giddy, like schoolgirls. Both little Barbie dolls they were – blonde hair, flawless skin, Barbados tan, and designer gear from head to toe.

"... so I said yeah that's totally cool, and he was like, yeah cool well I'll be in Renard's after the gig, so maybe I'll see you there, and then I snogged him for a bit, so we're definitely going in ..."

"Fuck yeah," said her friend, "I hope that other guy'll be there, he's so cute ..."

"Oh, it's just this house here please, with the hedge."

I turned in to the nominated house, a massive detached affair, and parked up in the driveway beside daddy's new gleaming new hundred grand car.

"Okay, I'll go in and get some cash from my dad. You wait here."

"Duh, what else am I gonna do? Hurry up, okay?" said her friend.

With that blond number one got out of the car, and as she ran over to her front door and disappeared inside, I reversed back a little bit to make room for my turn.

"Sorry, you couldn't turn on the light for a minute please, could you?" her friend asked politely.

"Sure, yeah," I agreed and flicked on the interior light.

"Thanks," she said, leaning forward to use my rearview

mirror to freshen up her make up and hair.

"You on the razz tonight, yeah?" I asked.

"You bet, and we so shouldn't be, have exams tomorrow. But they're not 'till the afternoon I s'pose ..."

"What are you studying?"

"I'm in Trinity," she answered.

She might have been cute, but she was also deaf. I had asked her *what* she was studying, not where she was studying, but she obviously felt that just saying she was in Trinity should suffice as an answer to my question.

"Right. Very good. What's on in Renard's tonight?"

"It's who's in there, not what's in there," she said, correcting me.

"Oh yeah? You on the pull?" I ventured.

"Totally. These guys we met in Lillie's last week are in there," she said, clapping her lips together, satisfied with her lipstick application. A quick brush of her long blond hair and she was happy. "Cool, thanks," she said, making a token effort to re-position my mirror in its original setting.

"No problem."

"Oh come on," she pleaded, looking back to see where her friend was.

"Relax, it's only gone twelve," I said.

"What? Oh no, it's not that, I'm dying for a pee!" she laughed.

"Oh, well I can't help you there, sorry."

She gave a little laugh whilst squirming in the back seat before saying, "Oh fuck it," and getting out of the car. I thought she was going into the house to use the marble-floored facilities with separate his 'n' her washbasins, but no, she strolls over to an evergreen tree on the other side of the driveway, lifts up her skirt, pulls down her knickers, squats down and does her business right there in the garden, not perturbed at all by the fact that she was directly in my field of illuminated vision. All done, she stands up, fixes her clothes and trots back to the car.

"Hope you washed your hands," I asked her.

"What? Oh yeah," she laughed, "I couldn't wait, I was dying to go."

"A house that big, you'd think they'd have a loo," I suggested.

"Don't want to wake her parents. They'll freak if they know we're going out," she explained.

"Oh right. I thought she was gonna get some cash from her dad though?"

"She is, she's … just, not going to tell him," she said, and then after a pause. "We're really bad, aren't we?"

"Nothing to do with me. I couldn't care less."

At last blonde number one appeared again, closing the front door gently behind her, before running over to the car.

"Okay, let's go," she said breathlessly, and I left the crime scene to head for town.

"Oh no, sorry, can you turn left here please?" she asked.

"I thought you wanted Renard's?" I said.

"Yeah we do, but I have to go to the petrol station first …"

"For what? What's up?" inquired her friend.

"I couldn't find any cash," blondie whispered in a clandestine fashion, "so I got a cheque instead. We'll go down to the garage and cash it, yeah?"

"Yeah, cool," agreed her accomplice.

"We have to stop in at a garage on the way. I'll show you where it is. We'll only be a minute, thanks. Do you have a pen I could borrow?"

"Yeah, alright," I said. Couldn't care less what little scam daddy's princess pulled as long as I got paid, so I handed over the pen and flicked on the light once again.

"Thanks a million," she said gratefully, and began her forgery, while her friend looked on encouragingly.

"Are you sure you can do his signature?"

"Oh yeah, I've done it loads of times, even showed mum how to do it!" she laughed.

I proceeded to the petrol station as requested and pulled up at the hatch where blonde number one got out to utter the forged cheque as her friend and I watched with vested interest. The transaction did not appear to be going too smoothly at first, with the store operator shaking his head forlornly behind the plate glass window, despite blondie's protestations of authenticity. It looked like the deal was shot, but then she played the spoilt-little-arrogant-bitch-from-hell card and the negotiations moved on apace.

"Look, do you see the name on that cheque? He happens to be a very good friend of XXXX XXXXXX who owns this garage, okay? We have a huge account here, and I don't think he'd be very happy to hear about this, right? But if you don't cash that cheque I'm gonna tell my dad to close the accounts and it'll be your fault, okay?"

What a fucking cow. Poor bastard in the shop relented and took the cheque from her and handed over the cash. Blondie turned around haughtily and marched triumphantly back to the car.

"See?" she said, fanning out the notes for her friend to inspect.

"How much did you get?" giggled her pal.

"Only ninety," she said. "He only looks at cheques for over a hundred really, and 'cos it's here, he won't even think about it, so it's cool."

"Cool! Let's go!"

Little adventure over, I pulled out of the garage and tore into town, depositing Thelma and Louise outside Renard's as requested, where they air-kissed Robbie on the door and sauntered in, every bit the belles of the ball.

Accounting for your movements

I was driving down Abbey Street a couple of months ago when two lads hailed me outside Spirit, the club in the now defunct HQ venue. They didn't look like your usual Spirit punters, they were the wrong side of twenty five, were dressed in an all too traditional manner, and sported no body jewellery or tattoos of any description. They seemed a bit lost and gratefully jumped into the car.

"Well that was a load o' bollix, twenty five euro down the bleedin' swanee there Pat," said the lad in the back seat.

"I know, I know Mick, now give it a rest, would ye?" answered Pat.

"Alright lads, where're you heading?" I interrupted.

"Alright pal? What'll we do Pat? D'ye fancy a pint or do you wanna go home?"

"'Course I fancy a pint, I'm not goin' home! Sure Jaysus, it's only gone twelve!"

"Right so, we'll head up to, ah, Break for the Border, yeah?"

"Ah no, dat's a kip dat is ..." complained Pat.

"Well, you think o' somewhere then, ye moany fuck. Up

towards the green please, pal, yeah?"

"No problem," I said, swinging down Liffey Street to get back out on to the quays.

"No crack in there, no?" I ventured.

Pat just looked at me mournfully and shook his head.

"No, not at all, not our thing, all bleedin' kids, and that poxy techno music beatin' the head off ye. I dunno how they do it, I really don't," said Mick.

"And what had you going in there in the first place?" I asked.

"Muppet there was raving on about some new club," continued Mick, gesturing towards Pat in the front, "Spearmint and Rhino he said it was, saw it in the paper, and that it was supposed to be off the wall altogether, all strippers and shit. So the two of us get a pass for the night from the ball and chain, and off we go ..."

"Look, I did read aboud it Mick," protested Pat. "I'm tellin' ye. Did you not hear about it bud, no? Thought you'd be well up on what's happenin' in town like ..."

"What did you say it was called?" I asked, smiling at his suggestion, "Spearmint and Rhino? Never heard of it. Funny name though, isn't it?"

"Yeah, I thought that alright, but I saw an article aboud it in de paper las' weekend, I know I did ..." continued Pat.

"Yeah well, that poxy place Spirit is the closest to it we got, as far as the name goes anyways. Load o' shite it was an' all," moaned Mick.

"And would you not head up to the likes of Angels, or that place Lapello, no?" I asked, smiling to myself as I crossed the bridge and went down D'Olier Street.

"Bin dere, dun dem," Pat assured me. "Anyway, before we start lashing inte de pints up here Mick, we better ged our story straight, don't want a repeat o' de las' time, when you hung me out te dry with Louise ..."

"What are you talkin' about ye gobshite? You hung me, sayin' we met up with John an' the boys, and then Jackie meets his missus down in bleedin' Tesco's and turns out he was off on a bloody golf do, ye moron ..."

"I did not. *You* were de one dat said we met up with John. Now don't start Mick ..."

"Like fuck I did Pat. Jackie knows I don't' even like the bollix. I'd hardly be goin' drinkin' with 'im now would I? Would ye cop on?"

"Yeah, yeah, whatever," said Pat dismissively, giving me the old he's-not-the-sharpest-tool-in-the-shed look. "We boat ended up hung anyways and we don't need a repeet of it, dat's all I'm sayin' ..."

"Yeah ... right," said Mick, shaking his head in disbelief. "So where were we?"

"Tell ye what, we went fer a bite te eat, and then we just went up te ... Sinnotts, yeah Sinnotts for a few pints, right? Food and then Sinnotts, *sin é*, yeah?"

"Fair enough so? Where did we go for food though?" inquired Mick.

"Oh Jaysus, do I have te think of everytin' do I? Where wood we have gone fer a bid o' grub pal?" Pat asked me, implicating me in their web of deceit.

"I don't know ... how about Milano on Dawson Street?" I suggested.

"Milano on Dawson Street, yeah? Yeah ... sounds good to me. D'ye get dat Mick? We were in Mi-lan-o, on Dawson Street, okay?" Pat intonated clearly.

"Yes I did, I'm not fuckin' deaf ye sap. What kind of food do they have in there? All pasta and pizza and that kinda shite isn't it?"

"Wood ye shud up, ye're makin' me hungry now!" shouted Pat.

I pulled in outside Break for the Border and totalled the meter, while the two conspirators argued over the degree of accuracy required with their alibis.

"I'm tellin' ye Pat, you don't know Jackie. That's how she does it see, catches ye out on the details, yeah? She knows I don't like bleedin' pasta, so she won't go fer that at all. No, we'll have te come up with somewhere else."

"Now, that's six forty please," I said, interrupting the strategy discussion.

"Jaysus, it's yer auld one Mick, not de bleedin' Gestapo! Fer fuck's sake!" said Pat, raising his eyes to heaven as he handed me a tenner.

"That's what she's like, I'm tellin' ye, her aul lad was probably in de bleedin' Gestapo!" reasoned Mick as he clambered out of the car.

"Now there you go, cheers, and this is for you," I said, handing Pat one of my chewing gum tablets with a smile, "I reckon it's as close to Spearmint and Rhino you're gonna get to tonight!"

"Oh yeah, very good, very good smart arse," says Pat nodding his head. "Here Mick, look," he says, opening the door to share the joke with Mick, "Mick? Spearmint and Rhino? D'ye geddit? Chewing gum. Spearmint and Rhino, yeah? Haaa, haaa, very good …"

"Come on you, ye muppet, would ye?" said Mick despairingly, giving me the he's-not-the-full-shilling look.

"Cheers lads, all the best," I said, as Pat popped the chewing gum in his mouth and hops out of the car, where Mick gives him a friendly slap around the head as they make their way into the pub.

Whilst recording this tale I decided, purely in the interest of research you understand, to investigate the veracity of Pat's claims that there was in fact a chain of exclusive gentlemen's clubs, trading as Spearmint and Rhino. Utilising the globe-spanning, all-inclusive powers of Google, I found out that there wasn't. But that there was indeed a US-owned chain of such establishments, trading under the name of Spearmint Rhino, who have a number of venues in the UK, the nearest one to Abbey Street being the one strategically located beside Heathrow Airport. The lads will need a very well worked out story to cover that particular trip.

Two eggs in a hanky

" Yes, ye fuckin' were!"

"No, I fuckin' wassen!"

"Ye fuckin' were!"

"I fuckin' wassen!"

You get the idea. And I'd heard all this, as indeed did most of the street, before they even got into my bloody car. It was a Thursday night about one am and I was first away from the rank on Dame Street. They were twisted drunk, of course. Staggered across the road without looking, got into the last taxi on the rank, where the fundamentals of the queuing system as practised by most civilised societies were explained to them by the driver, got out again, and staggered down towards my car.

"Is it yew, is it?" he asked, as if – God forbid – we were old school pals who hadn't seen each other in ten years.

"Is what me?" I replied, confusing the issue still further.

"Wha'?" he said.

"'Course it's bleedin' him, ye dope! D'ye see annieone else in front of 'im?" the peroxide blonde reasonably concluded.

"Who yew callin' a dope, ye slut!" came the reply.

"Shut fuckin' up, an' ged in will ye, be here all bleedin' nite!" she urged.

"Yew shuddup, I'll ged in when I'm ready te ged in!"

She was right; we could have been here all bloody night with this tit-for-tat exchange. I saw another couple approaching who looked eminently more preferable to this pair and hoped they would get into my car, but the driver behind me – quite wisely – urged them to get into his car, lest he be landed with the acrimony that was bound to develop with these drunken idiots. Your man eventually located the handle and yanked the door open, clambering in ahead of his by-the-looks-of-it-soon-to-be-ex-girlfriend. She sighed loudly and followed him, slamming the door after her in a suitably dramatic fashion.

"Where're you off to?" I asked curtly, figuring that the levels of intoxication I was dealing with would render any small talk both meaningless and exasperating and ultimately only further delay our departure.

"Donnamead, yeah?" blondie said, as if inquiring if such a place existed.

"Bollix te dat, I'm goin' home te me ma's. Darndale bud, yeah?" he countered with.

I took off down Westmoreland Street, heading for the North Strand, knowing at least that we were headed up the Malahide Road, and listened as the feuding parties thrashed it out between themselves.

"Cop on Steven, wud ye? We're goin' home, righ?" she said sternly, and then to me once again, "we're goin' te Donnamed, tanks."

"Right," I said quietly, perhaps not wanting Steven to think I was conspiring with his girlfriend.

"Lookit," Steven said, "I'm goin' te me ma's, righ? Not home wit yew, an' dat's bleedin' dat!"

"Why? Why're ye goin' te yer ma's? What's up wit ye?"

"Yew! You're what's bleedin' up wit me!"

"Whadave I dun?" she exclaimed in a shocked manner.

"Don't start dat Mandy, ye know well what ye dun! Fleartin' yer hole off wit dat prick!"

"Oh Jaysus, I told ye, I dun nuttin', righ?" Mandy protested.

"Me bollix! I seen ye! I seen ye fleartin' wid 'im ..."

"Oh fer fuck's sake Steven, he came over an' assed me if I wanted te dance wid 'im an' I said no, I didden, an' dat was it ..."

"Oh, but dat's it ye see, dat wassen it, wassen it not?" Steven said rather confusingly.

"Whadia talkin' about dat wassen it, dat was so bleedin' it!"

Steven manages to get himself into a semi-upright position to deliver his killer piece of evidence.

"I'll tell ye whad it was, I'll tell ye! He said yew were lookin' great, an' yew said," he shouted with pointed finger, "an' yew said, ye're not looking, too, bad, yerself! Dat's what yew said! Derek fuckin' herd ye!"

"I did in me bollix!" Mandy replied, mixing her genders if not her metaphors. "Don't mind bleedin' Derek, he's owney a stirrin' bastard an' yew know well 'e is. Yew know dat after all de shite in Majorka las' year wit him an' Katrin, righ'?"

"Whadia talkin' about poxy bleedin' Majorka fer? I'm talkin' about tonite in bleedin' Club M, an' yew givin' it lodes wit some faggit in a pink sheart!"

"I wassen givin' it lodes! An' whad if I was? Am I not allowed talk te annieone but yew, is dad it? Don't be so stewpid ..."

"Yeah, dad is it! Ye're supposta be me bird, yeah? Dat means ye talk te me, ye tell me I'm lookin' great, not some udder prick!" reasoned Stephen

I got the feeling Steven was the jealous type, and that alcohol – especially in large quantities – fuelled his insecurity. I wouldn't

169

have said that Mandy was a complete angel either, by any means, but I've seen this kind of thing a thousand times and it baffles me why anyone would go out with someone like this when they know that every time they end up in a nightclub, it's going to end up with the same acrimonious outburst about such alleged coquettish behaviour.

"Oh dat's it den, is it? Ye're jealous ..."

"No, I'm fuckin' delited dat meself an' Derek leave youse two alone fer two bleedin' minits te go te de jax, an' wen we come back, yer givin' it lodes te some knobend!"

"Wud ye ged a grip Steven," said Mandy. "I wassen givin' it lodes, Jaysus. Youse wear gone about half a bleedin' hour anyways so yis wear, dat lad probly tought dat me and Katrin wear on our own. Big bleedin' deal, nuttin' happened, I dunno why ye have te ged in a bleedin' snot aboud it an' ruin de nite ..."

"We wear onwney gone two minits, we went te de jax ..."

"Yeah, yis went off te de jax tageder an' all like two queers. I taut owney gerls wear supposta do dat! Did ye haf te hold his bleeddin' dick fer 'im an' all did ye?"

"Shut de fuck up yew, ye stewpid bleedin '..."

"Wipe his hole fer 'im, did ye?"

"Mandy, I'm fuckin' warnin' ye, shudup or I'll bleedin' burst ye!"

"Ye will, yeah."

There followed a brief recess as both parties regained their composure and planned ahead for their closing arguments. I had taken the decision to head for Donahgmede – working on the basis that the row, as had previously been the case in similar altercations between drunken couples, would be sorted out by the time we had reached their shared abode – and was now heading past The Goblet in Artane. I have to say I was enjoying this particular tiff. It was all very light-hearted, and quite entertaining really. Evidently, the dispute centred around an amorous advance allegedly made to Mandy by an as yet unnamed third party, and whether or not the manner in which such an advance was ultimately rebuffed by Mandy constituted a breach of the terms of their relationship, as set down by Steven, who was firmly of the opinion that Mandy – seeing as how she was his "bird" – should have eyes for him alone, and constantly accommodate his insecure tendencies by telling him he's great and not "sum udder prick". It should be borne in mind however that the validity or otherwise of Steven's allegation of such an infraction of said terms was based solely on the evidence of a close friend and confidante, Derek, and that the credibility of this witness had to be questioned in light of the "Majorka" incident. Mandy, in conducting her own defence, was proving that she was well able for Steven, and I suspected that this was one of the reasons he was attracted to her, another being that, to use the common parlance, she was "a fuckin' ride". As I waited to turn right on to Tonlegee Road, the session resumed.

"Lookit, I'm not sayin' dat yew started it, righ?" continued Steven, "but dis kinda shit happens evry time we go out. I go te de jax, or te get de gargles in, or whadever, an' I come back, an' dere's sum prick chattin' ye up. An' I've a pain in me bollix wid it …"

"I can't help it if sum bloke wants te chance his arm an' ask me up fer a dance, can I?" argued Mandy reasonably.

"Dance me bollix! Nobudy wants te dance wit ye Mandy. Dey want te ride ye, d'ye unnerstand me?" said Steven, explaining the ways of the world to the naïve Mandy.

"I'm not bleedin stewpid Steven," Mandy retorted. "D'ye not tink I kin stand up fer meself, is dad it? D'ye tink I want te go off an' do de durt on ye, is dad it? Well I don't, an' if I did, I'd at least bleedin' dump ye furst an' all! I've never cheated on annieone in me life."

"I know well ye kin stand up fer yerself Mandy," said Steven in a seemingly conciliatory tone. "It's jus' ... it's de gear ye wear luv, udder blokes wud look at ye and tink yew wear fair game, d'ye know whad I mean?"

"Oh so now I'm a slut, is dad it?" Mandy shrieked. "Whad is it wit yew? I can't do antin' rite fer ye! What's wrong wit dis?"

I glanced in the rearview mirror to independently examine the apparel now under scrutiny. For the evening wear competition, Mandy had chosen an all white ensemble – sheer trousers which looked as though they had to be sprayed on, and a matching halter neck top, completely bare at the back, and secured only by a flimsy strap which was tied up more loosely than a kindergarten boy's first pair of lace-up shoes. She definitely had the body for it, no doubt about that, and there are plenty of girls around town who regularly wear even more outrageous outfits than this, but in fairness I could see where Steven was coming from, given his own undeniable insecurities. At this point he slumped back into the corner of the seat. He looked uncomfortable at what had to be said, but he was going to say it nonetheless.

"Fer fuck's sake Mand, there's nuttin' wrong wid it as such," he sighed. "It's jus' dat it's all white, an', we wear in a nite club, yeah? Wit strobe lites, an' laser lites, an ..."

"An' wha'?" Mandy interrupted, "so bleedin' wha'?"

"Ah Jaysus Mand, ye've no fuckin' knickers on ye! I mean, evry bloke in dere was lookin' at yer fanny! It's jus' nod on, it really fuckin' issen ..."

"I don't believe dis! I don't fuckin' believe dis! Yew are in a snot wit me because of whad I'm wearin'? Are yew fer real or wha'?"

"Well, it's jus' dat, I mean, it's not nice fer me, seein' yew dresst up like dat an' den evry bloke sniffin' round ye like a bleedin' dog in heet! I mean, lookit Katrin, she wore a pair of black slacks an' a white blouse, an' she looked fine ..."

"Oh so now ye want me to wear the same ting as Katrin, do ye? D'ye want me te ring 'er before we go out an' ask 'er whad she's wearin', is dad it? Fer fuck's sake Steven, we're not Atomic bleedin' Kitten!"

Steven sighed loudly once again and shook his head in despair. I was doing my best to give them the space to sort things out, but once I turned left onto the Grange Road, I had to ask for directions.

"Ah, whereabouts do you want?"

"Wha'?" asked Mandy, as if surprised by my presence, and then realising where she was, "Oh yeah, wear are we? Ah, rite at de shoppin' centre, den yer sekind left, an' I'll show ye."

"Right so," I said.

The conversation resumed in a decidedly hushed tone, Mandy and Steven now, for the first time apparently, aware that I had heard every word of their delicate debate. Try as I did, I couldn't really make out what they were saying, but some sort of accord was obviously reached, judging by the markedly more dignified nature of the exchange. I followed directions as issued by the girl who chose to "go commando" and pulled up at the kerb. Steven sorted out the fare and then got out to follow Mandy who was waiting patiently on the footpath. As I was reversing to swing around, the pair ambled across the road, and it was really only then that I fully realised the cogency of Steven's argument. Mandy's firm, slender frame was brightly illuminated by my headlights, and what a sight it was. Like two eggs in a hanky, as they say. Minus the hanky practically.

Meeting

This particular anecdote returns to a subject touched upon in an earlier story – the one concerning the teenage girls attending Wesley. I referred briefly to the antics such girls and their male friends get up to before actually heading off to the disco or pub or wherever, and lest you think I was exaggerating, here's a tale from the front line – or back seat as it was – which should strike the fear of God into sex educators and parents of teenage girls and boys alike.

It was just gone half ten on an unusually pleasant Friday evening in December 2002. I had dropped off in Rathgar at the Orwell Lodge Hotel and instead of heading straight back into town, I decided to continue in a southerly direction, and head for the somewhat rarefied environs of the south county. As it gets towards eleven o'clock or so on a Friday and Saturday night, I try to make my way towards Blackrock and Dun Laoghaire, in the hope of accommodating the alcohol-induced transportation requirements of the sometimes-but-not-always better class of asshole that socialises and lives around these parts.) And so I headed down the hill past the nursing home, slowing down to lust after the new Range Rover parked outside that cool house built into the steep hillside. As I crossed the bridge over The Dodder, a young girl flagged me down earnestly. I pulled in and four teenagers piled into the car, all excited and anxious at the same time.

"Oh my God, thank you *so* much for stopping. We are like, *so* dead," shrieked the girl in the front seat excitedly.

"Can we go to Rathmines please?" inquired a decidedly more calm and older looking girl in the back.

"Yeah, no problem," I said, banging on the meter.

I swung the car around and took off back up the hill, glancing longingly once again at my Range Rover, wondering for a moment if I needed help, before shaking my head in disgust that such a thought had even entered my head.

The little one in the front, who possessed a lovely Jane Austen type name, which I better not repeat lest her parents are reading this, resumed her excited chattering. So let's call her Meg, and the other three Jo, Beth and Amy. Little women.

"Thank you *so* much, you saved my life just now," she said in a terribly grateful if somewhat overly dramatic tone, one which, nonetheless, I wished more of my passengers would adopt.

"Oh yeah? Why, what's up?" I inquired politely.

"My mom's coming to collect me at eleven and if I'm not in Jo's house, I am *so* dead ..." she confided.

"We've loads of time, Meg, it's only twenty to eleven," confirmed one of the others in the back.

"Jo? Can I just go into your house and wait in the hall and then come out when my mom gets there?" asked Meg, confidently displaying an ability for tactical planning which I was sure would stand to her as she got older and her dalliances became increasingly more complex.

"Yeah, cool," acquiesced Jo, fully understanding that the devil is indeed in the details.

"Who did you meet, Beth?" inquired Meg, turning round to her friends in the back.

"Gavin," revealed Beth, a skinny little blond-haired girl of about fourteen or fifteen.

(There's that word "meeting" again. Not quite sure how it arrived at its current position in the phraseology of the youth of today, but after having ferried any number of lusty young teenagers of both sexes home before curfew and ear wigged on their conversations, I certainly know what it means. "Meeting" concerns itself with the now quite common practice of young boys and girls – already friends on a platonic level – pairing off with each other to practise, by mutual consent, their respective "making out" techniques. Without being too graphic, this would consist of one party advancing from "first base" to howsoever far around the metaphorical baseball diamond they felt comfortable with, and their consenting partner then reciprocating the manoeuvres as practised by their sex. Sounds quite terrifying I suppose if you're a parent of one of these particular creatures. I'm not and don't ever intend to be, so it's probably a lot easier for me to say this, but in a way, I can see where they're coming from. Peer pressure is such a powerful force these days and it's only going to get stronger and stronger on younger and younger kids. Teenage taunts, especially those that can arise from being unpractised in the art of heavy petting, can, and often do, torment a young person for years to come. The way these girls saw it, better to face up to the inevitable courting rituals that are not far down the line and get yourself into a position where you can acquit yourself with some aplomb than to be ridiculed in the toilets or behind the bike shed for the rest of your secondary school years.)

"Oh Gavin's really nice," said Jo. "He's a great kisser ..."

"Yeah, really soft lips," added the fourth girl.

All speaking from experience, by the sounds of it. Gavin was certainly popular with the ladies, the jammy bastard. Jesus, I was no more snogging three cute chicks on successive Friday nights when I was his age. Where did it all go wrong? Having a few quid for a game of snooker down in the Dundrum Leisure Centre and avoiding getting beaten up by Mad Macker on the way home through the shopping centre was the height of my weekends. No wonder I'm "emotionally stunted" as my therapist says.

"What about you, Meg, who were you with?" Jo then inquired.

"Best night ever," declared Meg emphatically. "I was with Fiachra, it was *so* cool."

"Oh my God! Do you like him?" exclaimed Beth, leaning forward to get the gossip, both surprised and excited at the prospect that her friend could actually genuinely fancy the guy whose parents she had no doubt just saved the expense of a bi-annual visit to the dental hygienist.

"Yeah, he's so cute," Meg said. "And he's really sweet … wears cool clothes …"

"Yeah, I suppose so," agreed Beth. "So are you gonna see him again like?"

"Definitely, he's gonna text me on Monday and we'll meet up after school."

"Wow, that's *so* cool," said Jo. "What do you think of Stephen, Beth?"

"Stephen? He's really nice, like, but … I don't know if I'd like to go out with him or anything …" answered Beth.

"Why? I think he's really cute. And funny too …" argued the fourth girl, a little thing of about fourteen with long, dark hair in ponytails.

"Yeah, he is, but you haven't *met* him, Amy. He's … like, well when he was ..." countered Beth.

Four sets of eyes were then fixed in my direction. There followed a flurry of diplomatic looks and nods of heads that would make the hucksters in the Fianna Fáil hospitality marquee at the Galway Races look like bumbling, tactless amateurs, and then silence descended on the car. At this point we were heading in the definite direction of slumber party girl-talk and mine was clearly an obtrusive and unwelcome presence. Well tough shit, girls, you're not old enough to drive, so mine is definitely a wholly necessary – if decidedly obtrusive and unwelcome – presence. A mute consensus was reached that the next part of the conversation could wait until the girls were ensconced in the privacy of Jo's bedroom, and we progressed in silence.

At this stage we were passing Trinity Hall in Dartry, where McNamara & Co. were busily constructing a couple of hundred apartments for the students of Trinity College, and where, I mused quietly to myself, in just a few short years time, these same girls, judging by their accents, clothes, and residential addresses, would be "meeting" many, many more young men, only this time without the bothersome constraints of a curfew, which was now fast approaching.

As I waited to turn right at the lights, the girls reverted to tactics, and chewing gum was passed around.

"Would you like one?" proffered Meg politely.

I turned to see what was on offer and, my curiosity piqued, accepted a Wrigley's Extra Thin Ice, if you don't mind. Quite nice it was too, if a little zesty for my delicate palette. Ideal for eradicating the odour of foreign bodies on one's breath as one prepares oneself to be escorted home by one's *mater* or *pater*. And for alcohol too, I suspect. And so with the air in the car fresher than that of a cable car ascending Mont Blanc, I progressed past Brookfield Tennis Club to the shrill sounds of polyphonic text message alerts and excited shrieks.

"Oh my God, that's Fiachra!" declared Meg delightedly, scanning the screen of her top of the range Nokia.

"What's it say?" asked Beth curiously.

"Meg, what did he say?" further interrogated the blond-haired girl.

"Oh, just that he really enjoyed tonight and wants to know if I got home okay," replied Meg.

"That's *so* sweet," said Beth.

I was now on the wide, leafy road requested, and followed Jo's instructions to her house, where after totalling the meter and telling the four young ladies how much the fare was, there followed a spell of verbal arithmetic to determine each party's contribution that would have made their maths teacher blush with embarrassment. Finally, after a mammoth negotiating session chaired by Alan Greenspan, consensus was reached that €6.20 divided by four was indeed €1.55 each. Fluffy pink purses were produced and I was bombarded with a kilo of small change. Four thank-yous, four goodbyes and three door slams later, a peaceful, almost sleep-inducing, calm filled the interior of my Saab. I exhaled deeply and swung the car around, narrowly avoiding an oncoming Chrysler Grand Voyager which veered across the road without indicating. The driver parked outside the same Victorian red brick into which the four girls had darted only two minutes previously. A polite beep of the horn announced Meg's "mom's" arrival. God love her, the poor deluded woman. She probably thought the girls had spent the evening short-listing proposals for forthcoming science projects, discussing impending lacrosse engagements with St. Trinian's and how best to help the less privileged members of society, before deciding that a carol singing evening would be an ideal fundraiser. Oh well, ignorance is bliss, as they say.

The Cider House Rules

It was the night after St. Stephen's Day, and I was already tired as I left the house at about half eight. Went down through Harold's Cross, heading in the general direction of Supper's Ready, just off Camden Street, to get my dinner handed to me on a plate, the way I like it. (I've never cooked a meal in my life, and never intend to. In a list of activities that are a complete waste of valuable time during our short stay on this earth, cooking jostles for the number one spot with gardening, polishing shoes, and cleaning venetian blinds.) So there I was, sailing over the bridge on to Clanbrassil Street, eagerly anticipating my braised lamb steak with special mash and some civilised conversation with Kevin about what a shithole Dublin was rapidly becoming, when I see this one just past McKenna's frantically waving me down. She was doing the old drunkenly-slapping-an-eight-year-old-on-the-head thing, so on principle I should have gone straight past her, but what's the point in having principles if you can't contravene them when it suits you? And I am a taxi driver after all, and it's hard to drive past a punter. So I stopped, and in she gets, after a little girl of about seven or eight, who quickly scampered across the back seat to sit behind me.

"Ringsend please, mister," the little one said breathlessly, as if she was late for an appointment.

"Shuddup yew, don't mind her, we're goin' te Basin Street, righ?" slurred the woman in disagreement.

"No we're not, we're goin' home te Ringsend," countered the little one pluckily. "I'm not goin' up te dem flats wit yew ..." she protested.

"Yew'll do as yer fuckin' told, righ? Or I'll give ye a bleedin' box, now shuddup," instructed the woman, who I now feared was the mother of this little girl. She was in a right state – all dirty and dishevelled, eyes popping out of her recently beaten head, and drunk as a skunk – at half eight in the evening.

Yielding to parental authority, however unsuitable it appeared to be, I turned left at Leonard's Corner and headed towards Donore Avenue, trying to remember where Basin Street was. I had dropped people off there a couple of times previously and wasn't particularly enamoured with the place to be honest. Fact was I had only returned to taxi driving a few weeks previously after spending an enjoyable if somewhat stressful four months working on a feature film adaptation of James Joyce's *Ulysses*, and my previously replete knowledge of inner city Dublin had slipped to a certain degree. Basin Street, Basin Street. Canal basin. Dry dock behind James's Hospital, that was it. Down Donore, across Cork Street on to Marrowbone Lane, left on to Forbes Lane, right on to Pim Street, round the back of the brewery and we're there. Geographical crisis thus resolved, I focused my attention on the relationship between mother and child in the back of the car.

"Lookit, I don't want te go up te dem flats, an' sit dere watchin' yew drinkin' wit all yer winos, I want te ..."

"Lissen te me, we'll owney be up here fer a wile an' den we'll go down te yer bleedin' nana's gaf, righ?" mother replied, angling for the compromise solution.

"No! I don't want te go up dere! I'm not goin' in, an' ..."
further protested the little one.

The mother went to give her a dig but thankfully her
inebriated condition prevented her woefully underpowered strike
from finding its intended target, and she slumped down on to the
seat, laughing pathetically.

"Ah c'mere darlin'," she slurred, reaching out her hands,
expecting the gesture to be reciprocated.

"Ged away from me, yer stinkin'!" shouted the little one in
rebuttal, retreating further over to her side of the back seat.

Any playful notions quickly disappeared as the mother
narrowed her eyes and adopted a surly, paranoid, and self-
destructive look that was utterly bereft of any affection for the
cute little girl that was her daughter.

"Yew watch yer bleedin' moute yew, or I'll burst ye," the
mother said, regaining an upright position. "Don't yew dare
speak te me like dat, right?" she roared.

I could tell that such exchanges were the norm for this child,
and was totally freaked out for her. Imagine having to go through
this shit every day with your mother? And still be a kid as well,
trying to make friends at school and enjoy your hopscotch? Holy
shit, life's a bitch, isn't it? And a lottery as well. That could just
as well have been you or me born into those circumstances,
having to grow up in that kind of environment – no father figure,
and an alcoholic mother unable to take care of herself, never
mind a young child.

Dead silence in the car now for a minute or two, each
passenger staring blankly out their respective windows, avoiding
eye contact at all costs.

"Where de fuck are we? I don't reckinise dis place," inquired
the mother, trying to reinstate diplomatic relations.

"Dat's 'cos yer drunk, ye don't know antin' wen yer drunk, 'cos dat's what drink does to ye," replied the daughter matter-of-factly, revealing a knowledge of the perils of alcohol abuse that no child of seven or eight should be privy to.

I was expecting her reply to result in another attempted dig from the mother, but she let it slide, pretending not to hear it.

"Ah, now I know where we are," she said quietly to herself, as I turned on to Pim Street and the obviously familiar high walls and chimneys of the brewery came into view.

"Keep goin', yeah, 'round here," she said, urging me on towards the doss house where yet more cans of cider awaited her.

"Turn here now, yeah, go on down dere," she continued, pointing in the general direction of the car park in front of the flats.

I missed the turn in on purpose; preferring to stay on the road so as to effect a speedy exit once our business was done.

"Now, that's a fiver please," I said wearily as I pulled in at the kerb, half-expecting to be met with some excuse as to why she hadn't got any money to pay the fare. I couldn't have given a shit about the money to be honest, my head was spinning trying to decide what to do next. She was obviously in no fit state to be looking after this child, not tonight and not any night by the looks of her. I wanted to tell the little one to stay in the car and that I'd run her down to Ringsend to her granny's house after her mother got out, but how could I say that without causing another outburst?

"I taut yew said ye'd no money!" said the little girl in disgust as her mother produced a fifty-euro note, an excuse no doubt made earlier to avoid buying her a dolly or something she wanted. "Ye said ye didden ged antin' from dem," she said disappointedly.

"I diden, I had te borrey dis, righ?" the mother replied curtly, angry at having to explain her pecuniary situation to a child.

I took the fifty, checked its authenticity, and gave her forty-five change, figuring that, firstly, I was due it for services rendered, and secondly, it would be a fiver less she'd have to spend on booze. Either way, the little one wasn't going to see any of it, be it in the form of a new winter coat or a present from Santa.

"C'mon yew, hurry up," said mother, grabbing the change from me as she turned to open the door. The little girl moved gingerly towards the door, and then stopped and looked at me, as if disappointed in me by my lack of concern for her well being. She then turned to her mother who was now trying to stand up straight on the footpath without using the doorframe for support.

"I don't want te go in dere, gimme some money for the bus fare, an' I'll go home, an' yew can go in on yer owen," she suggested.

"Listen, you stay here, and I'll drop you down to your granny's house, okay?" I said quietly and quickly, before the mother copped on to the subterfuge at work in the car.

"What?" she said in an equally quiet voice.

"Just close the door, let her go, you stay here and I'll take you home," I said in an overly friendly voice, before realising that to this street-wise kid I probably sounded like some sicko paedophile trying to lure her away to some decrepit DV cam-equipped bedsit. She looked at me for a moment, rationalising the alternatives in her little head, before an arm reached into the car and grabbed at her.

"I said c'mon yew!" roared the mother, fretting that her fellow winos may have already made significant inroads into the stock of cans in the flat.

The little girl got out of the car, silently figuring that yet another night slumped on the floor of a dirty flat watching her mother drink herself into oblivion was a safer option than going off in a car with a complete stranger who may or may not bring her home safely. I sat in the car for a minute and watched as the mother walked impatiently towards the stairwell, the little girl lagging behind, wishing none of this was really happening. Halfway along the car park she stopped and turned around to wave at me. Not knowing what else to do, I summoned a smile and waved back at her. And then she was gone.

A pretty shit way to start a night's work.

Behind the Door

Thursday before Christmas of last year, and finally the festive bullshit, I mean revelry, seemed to have begun. A couple of years ago, once it hit the first week of December you'd be flying for the full month, coining it in. But then, there were only about 2,500 taxis out there, so there was obviously more punters per car available, whereas now there are 10,000 of us out there, so it has to be really busy for you to feel it. Not before time and all, you useless shower of bastards, I hear you say in cacophonous unison. Point taken, point taken, now kindly sit back down and breathe deeply. All I'm saying is that it was the nineteenth of December, and was only now beginning to feel a bit like the frenzied month it is supposed to be, okay?

Anyway, all over the city, people had casually gone to the pub for lunch and not bothered to return to the office for the afternoon stint, which was quite handy really, as it saved them the effort of having to walk back down to the pub again at half five. Only trouble was that as it approached midnight they could hardly walk at all. And so things were getting kind of messy. A young girl I had taken from The Wicked Wolf in Blackrock towards her intended destination off Tivoli Road in Dun Laoghaire had to get out a little earlier than expected, and throw up all over a very nice pre-owned Volvo V70 in the forecourt of JPS Motors. At least she had the decency to fling a tenner my way before she exited, resulting in a generous, if somewhat unintended, gratuity for yours truly, as the meter was only at €6.25 at that stage. That was the kind of thing we were dealing with – glorious gluttony, sheer abandonment, utter excess. And all in celebration of the birth of our saviour, Lord Jesus Christ.

A couple of hours later found me tearing down the quays on my way back from Stoneybatter. Going through the lights at Capel Street, two lads around The Morrison were waving quite frantically for a taxi, as if one of them were about to have a baby. None of my fellow drivers stopped, so I did, and the two lads piled in, one in the front, one in the back. Pure country, as they say – with a good amount of porter in them as well – but still sound nonetheless. No shite about them at all. Had a conversation started before their arses had made contact with their respective seats.

"Howiya goin' horse? Are ye well? I'd say yer quare busy tonight boy, ha? Tis fuckin' manic out there like!" said the lad in the front.

"Savage, boy, fuck-ing savage! Jesus, would ye get us home te fuck outa here?" echoed the lad in the back.

"Where are ye off to, lads?" I asked.

"Dun Laoghaire and then on te Dalkey, good man," replied the lad in the back, to my considerable surprise.

Dun Laoghaire and Dalkey, if you don't mind. Fair play to the boys, from the back arse of nowhere – outside of Dublin – and they land themselves in the prime residential areas when they come up. Gas isn't it? No dank bedsit in Rathmines or off the North Circular. I take off and continue on down the quays, listening as the boys discuss the events of the night just gone, which from the sounds of it had involved a great big gang of lads meeting up in a pub for their Christmas pints. The conversation quickly turned to the subject of the character of their many acquaintances, a topic as good as any I suppose as the year draws to a close and you're twisted drunk. The lad in the back went through a roll call of the people in question and the lad in the front then solemnly dispatched them to one of two groupings.

For some, obviously those whose loyalty and character was beyond question, the mere mention of their name was enough.

"Murph? Whad about Murph, ha?"

"Sound. Sound out," decreed the lad in the front, nodding his head slowly.

For others, obviously those whose loyalty and character was again utterly beyond question, but for all the wrong reasons, the mere mention of their name was enough.

"Oh hi, whad about the O'Connor fella?"

"Bollix. Pure bollix. If I never see that bastard again, it'll still be too soon."

And so it went on, and highly amusing it was too. I turned right over the river and tore down the deserted City Quay alongside the camp shires. (What are camp shires by the way? I reckon it's a nautical/stevedoring term myself, but remain open to correction. Answers on a postcard please, by last post on Friday, to the usual address.) As I went past the RDS down Merrion Road, the annual review had been completed and the conversation moved on to the subject of food.

"Any chance ye'd stop off at a chipper boss?" inquired the lad in the front.

I let out a trademark sigh – long, deep and heavy – to articulate my opposition to the idea. Stopping off at a chipper really bugs the shit out of me, can't stand it. You only have a window from midnight to four am to make your few quid in this game really, and the last thing you want to be doing is stopping off at some dump and waiting around while some lad full of drink negotiates a path through the police and paramedics on standby outside to order his alleycat burger.

"Would ye cop on to yerself Billy," said the other lad helpfully. "There's nathin open at this hour of the night. Can't ye fix yerself some tae an' toast when ye get home?"

"Ha? Why, what time is it?" asked Billy.

"It's half two. You won't get anywhere open at this hour out here," I said, gesturing towards the leafy enclaves of Ballsbridge, safe in the knowledge that, whatever about low standards in high places, one thing the good burghers of D4 simply would not stand for is a late night burger joint.

Billy mumbled something to himself sullenly, then perked up again and took out his phone as an idea came into his head.

"Who are ye callin' at this hour?" asked his pal.

"This wan I met the other week, fine thing – a nurse like, ye know?" replied Billy winking. Obviously the word "nurse" bore great significance.

"Oh yeah? Do I know her like?"

"No Redser, wouldn't think so," answered Billy. "She's a friend of one of the lads in the house like, only met her meself last Tuesday week when she called up. Went for a few pints with herself and the boys, had a right bit o' crack ..."

Redser continued his line of questioning in a suitably delicate fashion.

"Oh yeah? And did ye ride 'er?"

Billy chuckled and gave Redser a dirty big smile.

"Did I what! Fine thing she is, great goer ... She's a nurse like!" he said, repeating the nature of his latest conquest's profession.

It's nice to see some things don't change. When I was in college, myself and the lads used to regularly discuss the alleged voracious appetite for sex enjoyed by nurses, musing on its veracity. Brian (RIP) declared that nurses would be naturally more predisposed to casual sex than other females. When asked to fully clarify his position, he logically deduced that, surrounded everyday by suffering and death as they were, nurses were obviously of the opinion that one's own life could be cut short at any time by the cruel hand of fate and that it was best to enjoy it while you were able to. The rest of us nodded happily in agreement, concurring that he had indeed made a very strong argument. Shortly thereafter, numerous enquiries were made to determine the structure of the working week of student nurses and we then made it our business to be in Copper Face Jack's or McGowans when they were finished a week of nights and were out on the tear. We didn't enjoy a whole lot of success from such escapades mind you but it kept us entertained. Billy, on the other hand, seemed to have struck gold with this particular "wan", and was now making plans for a rematch. As he held the phone to his ear myself and Redser started laughing at his antics.

"Lads, lads! Would ye shush?" urged Billy, straightening himself up.

Redser smiled at me and nodded his head in Billy's direction, raising his eyes to heaven.

"Ye may pull in here for a minute horse, ye wouldn't know what this bollix is up to," he advised.

I duly oblige and pull in opposite the Merrion Centre while Billy cajoles his amour into letting him call around for a "cup of tea". Deal done, he smiles and puts the phone away.

"Could ye drop me over to Donnybrook for a few minutes and wait 'till I see how I get on?" he asks.

"Ah Jesus Billy," sighed Redser, "it's near three o'clock in the mornin' boy. Whad are ye doin' goin' over there at this hour?"

"She said I could call over, what d'ye expect me to do?" replied Billy incredulously. "I'll pay for the extra bit like, don't worry. If it's on, ye can go on home and I'll get a taxi later on ..."

"Are ye in work in the mornin'?" asked Redser.

"Ha? Sure I'm not goin' in there te fuck, are ye mad? Yer not goin' in either I hope, are ye?" asked Billy, stupefied at the mere thought of it.

"I am, yeah, I've a few bits to do like ..." said the diligent Redser.

"Well good luck te ye so, I'm away te get a ride. Lookit, here's twenty euro. Now that'll more than cover me goin' over to Donnybrook, right?" reasoned Billy.

"Yer some bollix, d'ye know that?" said Redser, snatching the note from Billy's hand, "c'mon so te fuck."

"Sound, sound. Donnybrook it is," Billy said to me cheerily.

I swung the car around and turned up Ailesbury Road, heading for Billy's love nest.

"What's the address?" I inquired as I turned right at the lights at the bus garage.

"Jesus, I haven't a notion, I was rotten drunk the last time I was here, hang on now 'till I get me bearings," answered Billy as he scanned the area for familiar landmarks. Eventually, he found it. "Oh yeah, it's down here, ye can turn here," he said.

I turned as directed and drove slowly down along the row of Victorian red brick houses.

"What number is it Billy?" asked a by-now somewhat exasperated Redser.

"How the fuck should I know? I was only here the once before like, and I was looking for a ride, not to send her a shaggin' postcard!" answered Billy impatiently. "Oh look, her fucking car," he said a moment later, "that's the one, she was shitein' on

about her new car alright. This is it, right, stop the car, I'm goin'
in ..."

"Go on so, ye gobshite," taunted his pal. "We'll stay here an'
have a laugh."

Billy checked himself quickly in the mirror and nodded
silently, obviously satisfied with what he saw. He turned to
Redser to issue instructions.

"Now no acting the bollix Redser, fair's fair, right?" Billy said
sternly, as if to imply that he would accommodate and support
him were the situation reversed and it was Redser who was about
to go and bang down the door of some poor nurse he had met
only once before.

"Jesus Billy, it's nathin to me either way. We'll give ye one
minute to get inside and then we're off outa here te fuck, right?"
replied Redser.

"Right so, good luck, I'll talk to ye tomorrow," said Billy
confidently. "Ye off down home, ye are? Sure, we might get a few
pints in first, ha?"

"We might, now would ye get away te fuck!" shouted Redser
hurriedly.

I went to move off as soon as the door was closed, but Redser
tapped me on the shoulder and urged me to wait a second.

"Hang on for one second, horse, will ye? I want to get a look
at this wan, see what class of a yoke she is at all ... nurse, ha?
There'll be some shlaggin' down home over this I can tell ye," he
said, laughing to himself.

I could see a light on in the hall through the fanlight as Billy
rapped gently on the door. After a minute or so, the nurse
appeared, opening the door only a fraction at first. As
negotiations moved along apace though, Billy finally gained
access to the pleasure palace and gave the two of us a victorious
smile as he closed the door behind him. I took off and headed for
Dalkey out along the dualler.

"Did you get a good look at her, did ye?" Redser asked me.

"Not really, no," I answered. "What did you make of her?"

"Dunno now, didn't get a right look at her either ... seemed a bit big alright though ..." mused Redser, somewhat unkindly perhaps.

"He's a gas man, isn't he?" I said, nodding my head backwards in the direction of Billy's love nest, quite admiring his neck and tenacity.

"That lad?" replied Redser. "Who're ye telling? He's some buck alright now, wouldn't be behind the door atall atall when it comes te getting his end away. He's pure legend at home like, there wouldn't be a young one for miles around he hasn't had a crack at."

Behind the door ... that was a good one alright. I laughed at his expression and we continued chatting, talking shite about Christmas etc. when he noticed my recently installed stereo.

"Hi, is that a Sony, it is, yeah?" he inquired. "Which one is it?"

"Couldn't tell you to be honest. It was the right money though, so I got it thrown in a few weeks ago, the other piece of shit was doing my head in. Great sound off it," I said, cranking up the volume on track nine – Pounding – of my Doves CD to illustrate.

"Mighty, Jesus, yeah, mighty. I got one for the girlfriend for Christmas d'ye see?" he explained. "She's been banging on about the yoke in her aul car, and I'd say that's the same one now, looks very like it ... so yer happy enough with it, y'are?"

"Ah yeah, grand job, better than the poxy radio at this time of night anyway," I replied.

"You're a fair bit out, aren't you?" I suggested as I drove down Mount Merrion Avenue. Nosy bastard that I am, I was fishing for info to ascertain what led him to be residing in Dalkey.

"Ha? Oh yeah, well I'm only up for about six months like, with the job, ye know. Back to college then, so I wasn't goin' arsin' renting a flat for that lent o' time like, so I'm stayin' with the granny out here …"

"Oh right yeah, that makes sense alright," I said, my curiosity sated.

"Ah sure it's grand like, ye know? Sure rentin' up here is crazy money boy. Dunno how people manage at all …"

Next thing, his phone rings, and he checks the screen to see who it is before answering.

"Oh Jesus help us! It's that bollix Billy! Isn't that gas? Now, eider she threw him out or he *is* the one minute man we're always shlaggin' him about!" he says to me, breaking his shite laughing.

"Hallo?" he says, as if not knowing who's on the other end of the line. "What? Who's this? Ah Billy, howiya? Jesus boy, that was fassth work alright! Ye all done, are ye?" Redser says, ripping into Billy and enjoying every second of it.

"Ha? Not at all, no chance, sure I'm home now meself," he lied, as I conspiratorially turned down the volume on the stereo to assist in the deception.

"No Billy, sure amn't I after tellin' ye I'm home? How can I go back for ye, ye gobshite? Yeah, well, hard luck boy, ye may get yer own taxi now, good night to ye!"

He puts his phone away and falls back on the seat, creased up laughing.

"Oh I tell ye, well if that doesn't bet all! She's after throwin' him out, sayin' he was in a right sstait, an' that all he was after was a ride! And then d'ye know what he says to me? Turn the taxi round an' come an' get me! Pure bollix like, isn't he?"

Though not wholly surprised at the outcome of Billy's drunken endeavours, I too was roaring laughing at the thoughts of the poor sod being turfed out of the house into the night. I pulled in as requested on Barnhill Road and Redser settled up with me, Billy's disproportionate, lust-driven contribution of twenty euros going most of the way to clearing the sum owed.

Takes two to tamango

One of the Christmas nights of 2002 found me out in the unfamiliar surroundings of Malahide. I had dropped off three people in various locations, finishing up on the rather coolly named Texas Lane. Decent punters, no agro, and a generous tip to boot. Covered my petrol money in one go – lovely. I find that there's never really anything happening out around these parts until midnight on a Friday or Saturday night and normally head straight back into town down the Dublin road, but being Christmas, I thought I'd shoot through the village and see what was going on. And lo and behold, it was hopping, people swarming around the crossroads looking for taxis. Did a few handy local hops, politely explaining that I lived in Bray and was rarely out around these parts and would thus have to be carefully directed every step of the way. That was a complete lie of course. I had moved from Bray some months ago and was now actually living in Terenure, but Bray sounded a lot more distant, probably because it was, and people were therefore less likely to start mouthing off about how I'm supposed to know where I'm going, the gobshites. It's amazing really, how put out some people are at the fact that you don't know exactly where they live, as if the most expeditious route to their own poxy house was itself a question in the PSV test.

After about an hour or so I had been to such delightful places as Biscayne, Seabury, Ard na Mara and Seapark, delivering people in various states of inebriation safely home. The more coherent of them had informed me that the night in question was the night of Gibney's Christmas party, thereby explaining the unusual numbers in the village. Apparently, pints were only €2.50 all night, instead of the usual €14.80 or whatever they are now.

Later on, as I was cruising down the coast road back towards the village, a group of people flagged me down outside the rather grandly named Grand Hotel. The back door opened and a cute blond girl of about twenty-five hopped in, followed by a guy of about the same age. I thought that was it and was about to pull off when he told me to wait, that there was one more to come. We were then joined by another blond-haired girl, who got in the back as well.

"I thought you were going back to Darren's with the rest of them?" asked blond number one.

"Eh, no I thought I'd go on home, I'm really tired. You're going on to Portmarnock anyway aren't you, Stephen?" blond number two said.

"I am yeah, it's cool. Shona's working tomorrow like," replied Stephen, gesturing towards blond number one, implying that if she wasn't working tomorrow, he would be stopping off at her place to make sweet love. Shona was, I suspected, a little miffed at having to share a taxi home with gooseberry blond number two, whose presence in the taxi stymied her opportunity to get a little loving in with Stephen on the way home.

"Oh right, fair enough," Shona then said. "Seapark first please."

"No problem," I said, and took off like a Malahide veteran for the short trip back to the estate I had just left.

"Have you got some cash for this, babe?" enquired Stephen of Shona as I turned right into Seapark.

"Jesus, I could have walked home for nothing, and now I have to pay for you to go to Portmarnock as well? What are you like?" she said, half annoyed, half taking the piss.

"Oh don't be like that, hon," said Stephen playfully, leaning over to kiss Shona. She laughed and pushed him away gently.

"Get off me you idiot, ah, it's a right here and then left and I'm about half way up."

"Right so," I replied and proceeded as directed.

"Are you going out tomorrow night, Sho?" enquired blond number two.

"Ahm, I don't think so, office party tomorrow night. Free bar as well, so I'll probably be wasted … why, what are you up to?"

"Oh nothing much, might stay local for a few beers, that's about it."

"Right, well I'll call you tomorrow, okay? Ahm, just here on the left is fine, thank you."

I pulled in at the kerb and watched in the rearview mirror as Shona gave her pauper boyfriend a tenner for the taxi fare. He smiled gratefully, and leant over to kiss her. She reciprocated enthusiastically and they proceeded to snog for a minute or two.

"Right, have to go," she said to Stephen.

"Okay cool, night babe," he replied casually.

"See ya. Bye Lorna, talk to you tomorrow."

"See you Sho, bye, take care," said Lorna, leaning over to give her friend a peck on the cheek.

Shona exited the car and as I swung around I asked where we were heading to next.

"Down to Wheatfield. Do you know it?" asked Lorna.

"Never heard of it," I answered candidly. The only Wheatfield I knew was the prison in Clondalkin. From driving along the Cloverhill Road you understand, not from having enjoyed the hospitality there. (Although, come to think of it, the bravura opening scene of my auspicious debut short film, *The Black Suit* – shamefully ignored by the jurors at various national and international film festivals I hasten to add – was filmed there.)

"Okay, it's back out on to the coast road and down towards Tamangos," advised Lorna helpfully.

"Grand, no problem," I said as we left the estate.

As we headed down the dark coast road I heard the sounds of frantic fumbling in the back of the car. I looked in the mirror, and to my utter amazement, there was Lorna, close friend of Shona, wearing the face off Stephen, current boyfriend of Shona! Holy shit, what a set up. Girlfriend only out of the car two minutes and you're stuck into her best mate! What an asshole. Now fair enough, both girls were very cute, and you'd be hard pressed to choose between them if you were lucky enough to be given the chance, but at the same time, it's not cool really is it? You're going out with one girl, you either stick with it and make the best of it, or drop her and head off to pastures new, but carrying on with her friend behind her back – literally – is not on. Takes two to tamango of course, and Lorna, the sultry temptress, was as much to blame. Not that those were the thoughts going through either Lorna or Stephen's head at this precise moment in time, no, not by a long shot. They were going at it goodo, determined to make the most of their precious time together. I thought it best to keep my own views on the situation to myself and continued down along the coast road in silence. Once I got to the Martello Tower though, I had to check which turn we were taking, though judging by the heated state of affairs in the back of the car I don't think either the infidel or the harlot would have minded if I continued on into town, did a quick loop of Stephen's Green and headed back out again before interrupting them. But I couldn't be arsed with that.

"Which turn is it?" I said quite loudly.

No response. Assholes. Now, I'm sorry, but I don't care how intense a lover someone may think they are, or how elevated their tantric state is whilst they are necking with somebody, as far as I am aware one's sense of hearing is in no way impaired, so I hit the brakes and came to a sudden halt just opposite Tamangos.

"What the fuck?" Stephen said irritably, as he disengaged from Lorna's tonsils.

"Which, turn, is it?" I repeated slowly, and in a rather psychotic tone. Must have been the water nearby, bringing out a Cape Fearesque quality in me. Whatever it was, it had the desired effect – Lorna sat up straight and assumed responsibility for the navigation.

"Okay, right, sorry. Where are we? Let's see … oh yeah, your next right here please, and follow the road around to the right …"

"Hey, c'mere …" said Lothario, trying to resume battle with Lorna's oesophagus.

"Stephen, stop, I'm nearly home …" answered Lorna, resisting temptation.

"I know, so c'mere …"

Oh God, that was scary. He sounded like Joey on Friends taking the piss out of Joey on Friends. This guy really was something else. Quite what he was I didn't know exactly, apart from an asshole obviously.

"Ahm, just here, thank you," said Lorna.

"Right so," I said, pulling in to the kerb and quickly checking the mirror to see what way they would leave things.

"Okay … bye … ah … listen, I don't know about …"

continued Lorna, until Stephen lunged at her again.

"What? Don't worry about it, c'mere," he said as seductively as a wetbag asshole like him could.

Lorna's resolve faltered momentarily and they were at it again, in it up to their necks, if you pardon the pun.

"Okay, no, stop Stephen, stop ... listen, this isn't fair, we have to stop doing this ..."

"Why? Nobody's getting hurt, we're just having a good time baby. It's cool."

"Shona's gonna find out sooner or later. And even if she doesn't, it's not right."

Noble sentiments my dear, however late in the day it was to be having them.

"Look, I have to go, okay? Bye," Lorna then said, getting out of the car quickly in case she fell under Stephen's utterly mysterious spell once again.

"Where are you off to?" I asked as the door closed.

"What's that?" Stephen said, smiling smugly at me and pretending he hadn't heard what I said, wanting to savour his moment of glory. "Oh yeah, back out of here man, and I'm just a bit further down the coast."

"Right so," I said, checking the meter as I turned around. Lorna didn't give him any money, and Shona had only given him a tenner, and the meter was now at €8.50 plus €1.00 extras.

"Have you got money for this, yeah?" I enquired.

"What? Yeah, it's cool, why, how much is it now?" he asked as I arrived back on to the coast road.

"Just over a tenner," I replied.

"Oh shit man, that's all I have ... I'm not that far down ... you wouldn't run us down would you?"

"Not if you don't have enough money, sorry," I answered, pulling in abruptly and totalling the meter while switching on the light.

"No? Oh man, that's bad form, it's only down the road like …"

"Well it won't take you long to walk then, will it?" I said logically, "and don't talk to me about bad form, you dickhead."

"What? Jesus man, chill out will you?" suggested Stephen, obviously still caught up in some West Coast vibe.

"That's a tenner please," I said resolutely.

"Fine, there's a tenner. Merry fucking Christmas."

"And a happy new year to you," I said cheerily, taking the tenner from him.

Normally I would always drop somebody to their door if they were short a few cents, but not that asshole. Stephen got out and slammed the door behind him. I smiled somewhat childishly to myself, turned left and headed back past Tamangos to the village to see if there was anything left up there.

Tactics

Talented as I am, clairvoyance is not my forte, so as you read this (in October 2003 if the PR thing went well and you're an early adopter), I don't know if the situation has worsened or improved, but at the time of writing this particular section of the book (January 2003, but don't tell my editor that – I'm supposed to have it finished in two weeks and I've another 12,000 words to do), relations between some of the old timer taxi drivers and new plate owners had soured to some degree. At least that's been my experience. (Don't get me wrong now, most taxi drivers work hard, doing their best to provide for their families and all that. And I'm sure most of them are nice enough lads as well, it's just that I don't know any of them personally at all. I just do my thing on the mean streets and go home. I don't drink tea or coffee so I've no business hanging around in Spar on Baggot Street for a chat, and since I got my own plate sorted out I haven't bothered with a radio either, so I have no contact whatsoever with other taxi drivers, other than the occasional exchange of verbal abuse when one of them snatches my fare, or *vice versa*, but what the hey, it's very competitive out there these nights with ten thousand of us floating around the city trying to make a living.)

You see, the problem is that a lot of these lads – some of whom may have paid as much as £100 for a plate many moons ago – think that their longevity in the business somehow entitles them to be an asshole. And ever since the long overdue deregulation of the industry, these assholes have been increasingly antagonistic towards some of the new entrants to the business. I say new, but in fact most of them, myself included, would have been renting an "old" plate or car for a good while and merely taken advantage of the opportunity to get our own cars and plates sorted out and make a living for ourselves instead of continuing to line the ever deepening pockets of the two or three lads who controlled the taxi rental market, and were at one time grossing in the region of £25,000 a week from such activities. Also, a good number of the "new" plates would have been taken up by long serving hackney drivers who could now legitimately stop on the street for punters, as opposed to furtively snatching them as they had done for years, having kitted out their cars with sixteen aerials adorned with table tennis balls and fishing floats so as to heighten their visibility to the public. And that's all dandy as far as I'm concerned, I've no problem with the increased number of taxis on the streets, though I do think the process could have been managed better, on say, an incremental basis, with fifteen hundred or so new taxi plates issued every year, rather than the overnight opening of the floodgates "solution" implemented by the gobshites in our local government. And now they're up in arms about their "decimated" livelihoods. Decimated my arse, as Jim Royle would say. The next time you're out driving around certain neighbourhoods on a Friday or Saturday night and you see a taxi parked up in the driveway, have a good look. Chances are the house will be the best presented in its immediate surroundings, with cobble lock driveway, new windows, aspirational Doric columns supporting the porch extension, and a new Nissan Micra for her indoors. These lads have been milking it for years and have nothing to worry about. I do accept fully, however, that there are some lads out there who might have used a redundancy payment to buy a plate, or re-mortgaged the house to buy one, but hey, tough shit, that's life. In the market economy, nobody owes you a living. You take a punt on something, if it works out, great, and if it doesn't, hard luck, dust yourself off and try again, but don't come the bleeding heart to me because I've no time for that shit at all.

The preceding little soapbox monologue is not just a self-indulgent rant, though it does feel good to get it down on paper. No, it serves as an introduction to this next little anecdote. The first part of it at least, in that it's something of a double header, with two separate incidents – which occurred on the same night as a matter of fact – coupled together (coupled together? Is that tautological?), to illustrate the two distinctly different tactics I employ when dealing with the assholes I encounter as I ply my trade on the mean streets of Dublin. One is decidedly verbal, while the other is more acquiescent and only inwardly verbal. We'll deal with the decidedly verbal technique first.

A Sunday it was if I recall correctly, and I was in the Maxol garage in Harold's Cross getting petrol. More accurately, I was *trying* to get into the Maxol garage in Harold's Cross to get petrol. Great value petrol in there it is too. (82.9 per litre of unleaded at the time of writing, which compares very favourably with those other thieving bastards who saw fit to charge 90 cents and more for a litre of the same poxy petrol.) The only trouble is access and sometimes subsequent egress. The pumps are not terribly well laid out, but I suppose it's the best he can do on such a small site. Whatever about the infrastructural deficiencies it might suffer from, this particular petrol station does have many other compensating benefits, such as being open twenty-four hours, a central location, highly efficient and polite staff and the practically unique facility – in this justifiably increasingly security conscious crime-ridden shithole of a city – of allowing customers inside the shop at all times. So anyway, there's me, trying to get at the pump, and parked in my way, right outside the door to the shop, blocking access to two pumps, is this piece of shit taxi with one of the "old" plates on it. I glance inside the shop to see if there's any sign of its owner appearing and there I see him, great big bastard sipping his tea having a look at the naughty bits in *The Daily Sport*. No sign of him moving along, so I give a good blast of the horn. He looks out at me in utter disgust, shocked and appalled that I, an upstart new entrant in the industry, would have the gall to summon him to his car in such an unruly fashion. He continues reading the paper for another minute or so, and I give another serious blast of the horn.

"What's yer bleedin' problem ye pox?" he shouts at me, stomping across the forecourt like Godzilla.

"Your poxy car is my problem. Now shift it, will you?" I replied.

"I'll move it when I'm good and ready to fuckin' move it, alrigh'?" came the response to my entirely reasonable request. "I was payin' for me bleedin' diesel, d'ye mind?"

Ignorant bastard he was, and a liar to boot, as the CCTV cameras in the shop would no doubt attest to, were they called upon as evidence, illustrating that the position his car was parked in could not have facilitated the delivery of fuel from pump to tank.

"No you weren't, you were reading the paper! Now move, it's not a fucking library!"

"Yew lookin' for a fat lip, are ye?" he threatened.

Now he was a good six foot tall, and was, thanks to the weekly consumption of about fifty pints of Uncle Arthur's finest, a huge fucker, but his sort are all bluff and bluster at the end of the day. At least, that's what I was banking on at any rate.

"No, I'm looking for some petrol. Now piss off and stop annoying me ..."

"It's youse dat has dis game ruined!" he shouted at me, reckoning, incorrectly, from my plate number that I was not long in the business.

"What are you talking about, you sap! It's ignorant fucks like you who ruined it for yourselves, holding everyone to ransom for years ..." I countered.

His argument was that I, and others who had bought a "new" plate, were personally responsible for the reduction in the value of his plate, and that the altogether more honourable thing to have done was to keep on paying through the nose to rent a taxi, thereby allowing him and his cohorts out in the airport maintain the *status quo* which facilitated them working as little as possible and playing pitch and putt as much as possible.

"Go on, yer nuttin bud a bollix!" he came back with, unable to defend his indefensible position.

"I'd hate to think what that makes you so," I finished with as he lowered his hulking carcass into his smelly car and drove off, blasting his horn at me as he went. I parried with the raising of a single digit and a smile and progressed, finally, to the pump to fill up with good value petrol.

So, you see, quite verbal there in that situation. Confrontational too, I suppose, but justifiably so, given the context of the incident, I think. Now we move on the second tactic – the more inwardly verbal one – which is deployed any number of times every night of the week, in the interests of a quiet life. You will know by now that the majority of punters in my car have consumed alcohol. That's why they're in my car in the first place I suppose, and abiding by the old rule of not biting the hand that feeds you, I generally don't bother getting too hassled when they start acting the gobshite, talking shit and giving me grief. I just drive faster and get rid of them as quickly as possible.

Now, as you will also know, I rarely initiate a conversation with punters in my car unless I have an idea they might be either entertaining to some degree, or actually decent old skins, and that doesn't happen too often. When people are drunk, however, a lot of them become quite paranoid, and they assume – quite correctly – that my silence is in fact some sort of judgement on them, and consequently can sometimes become quite aggressive. In recognition of this I find that the easiest thing to do is to conduct a two-tiered conversation with them, which works like this.

On one tier we have the verbal acquiescent conversation, which consists of me placating them with utterly meaningless and non-committal contributions, such as "Oh yeah", "Really?", "I know, I know" or "You're dead right", randomly interjected into the conversation. "You're dead right" is far and away the best one though, and I'll tell you why. It's universally accepted that "you" is one of the most powerful words in the English language as it involves the other party directly in the conversational exchange. Think about it. You're talking to someone and they say, "I love me". Not that interesting really, regardless of how life-affirming it may sound, but if they say, "I love *you*", then you're interested. Or scared, if the person saying it is a gym teacher in a private school and you're a heterosexual teenage boy who happens to be the last one in the showers. Either way, you're definitely involved in the conversation. (If you're curious, "love" and "free" are two more such words, for obvious reasons.) Saying "You're dead right" to someone who's pissed and to whom you're not really listening is great because, firstly, it assuages them and reinforces the drunken delusional stance they have taken on whatever topic they are babbling on about – thus quelling potential aggression – and because secondly, it sounds like you're actually listening intently to what they're shiteing on about in the first place.

Then on the second tier, we have the non-verbal element of the conversation, which consists of me silently saying to myself what I would really like to say to the asshole bending my ear at that particular point in time. This tactic is best illustrated with an example, so here goes.

A couple of hours after the altercation with my fellow taxi driver in the Maxol garage, I found myself up around Tallaght. Sunday nights can be fairly busy up there, with most of the pubs doing four hour-long happy hour promotions. I had dropped a lad off in Verschoyle in Citywest and was coming down the Blessington road when I got a fare down to the Plaza hotel. As soon as I dropped off there, three lads who had been refused entry for wearing beige instead of black socks or some such pathetic infraction of the bouncer code hopped in, deciding to try their luck down in the village. Only around the corner, but what the hell. Shot down there and dropped them off, and was heading away when this guy in leathers walks solemnly towards the car, motorcycle helmet in hand. He gets in the front and says he wants to go up towards Jobstown. Didn't like the look of him from the word go, but a fare's a fare, and I didn't want to break the nice little groove I had fallen into, so off we went.

"Leave dat dere now, it'll be safe 'till the mornin'," he said wearily, as though he had just travelled six hundred miles on it to get pissed, pointing at his motorbike.

"Yeah, you're right too," I said disinterestedly. (Do I look like I give a fuck about your poxy motorbike?)

"I'll leave this in de back if you don't mind, save me holdin' on to it," he says, turning awkwardly around to deposit his helmet on the back seat, swinging it wildly through the air as he does so.

"Fair enough." (Take my head off with the thing, why don't you.)

All's quiet for a minute and then head the ball, who was fairly pissed, starts muttering away quietly to himself, righting the world's wrongs in his own warped little way.

"So, what d'ye do with all yer money?" he says bitterly to me through partially gritted teeth.

"What?" I said. (If you just said what I think you said, you can go fuck yourself, asshole.)

"I said, what d'ye do with all yer money?" he repeated, as if he was an investigator working with the Criminal Assets Bureau.

"Pay my bills, same as everyone else," I replied vaguely. (What's it to you what I do with my hard earned money, you sap?)

"Yeah, very good, everyone pays deir bleedin' bills. I mean with the rest o' yer money, and don't tell me ye don't have any, 'cos I know ye do," he continued.

"Yeah, well there isn't much left after that," I offered, seething at the neck on the guy.

"That's bollix, I know loads of lads in dis game, and dey all have plenty of money. What d'ye do with yer money?"

"Do you? Well, good for them, I must be doing something wrong then, 'cos I don't, okay?" I said frostily. (Mind your own business, you sad, pathetic little bastard.)

He lets out a big, weary sigh – though nowhere near as good a one as I can muster up – and extends his hand in reconciliation.

"Let's start again," he says. "Me name's Mick."

[This bit isn't part of my two-tier conversation, by the way. That's why it's contained within these more structural looking parentheses as opposed to the elongated ones you should by now be used to. I just want to discuss a separate, though related, matter first. I hate that phrase, "Let's start again". It's so stupid, it's like when a judge in a murder trial says, "The jury shall disregard that last statement". How can you disregard that last statement? You just heard it, and if there was an objection submitted, causing the judge to instruct you to disregard it, it was obviously juicy information, so you're not going to disregard it, try as you may; it will linger in the back of mind during your deliberations, your subsequent procrastination possibly necessitating – at the taxpayer's expense – an overnight stay in a three star hotel, whilst you and your fellow jurors wrestle with the evidence put forward by the prosecution and the arguments offered by the defence, weighing it all up And at the back of your mind is that information you were instructed to disregard, but you can't. And so, you *re*garding that information you were told to *dis*regard, could tip the scales of justice and send an innocent man to jail. Or allow a crazed psychotic killer to walk free, depending on the nature of the information you were instructed to disregard. And so it was in this case. Mick had made his opening submission, which had not been well received. And so, appointing himself as judge, he had effectively instructed me to disregard his opening statement and requested that we "start again" so he could present himself in a better light. No way. I had taken the information on board, assimilated it, and arrived at the reasonable, and to my mind, wholly correct, conclusion that this guy was a complete asshole. I meet about a hundred and fifty people a week, and consider myself to be a very good judge of character, and nothing he could possibly say from here on in was going to change my mind. That's why "Let's start again", along with "The jury shall disregard that last statement", are such pathetic things to say, compounding and reinforcing, as they do, one's initial suspicions as to the nature of a person's character.]

"Alan," I lied, pretending not to see his proffered hand. I've only got two hands anyway, and they were both busy, one holding a cigarette and the other one steering the car through a roundabout.

"D'ye mind if I smoke, Alan?" he enquired.

"Work away," I answered politely. (You can smoke heroin for all I care, if it makes you shut the fuck up.)

Mick lights his cigarette with his Zippo lighter, drawing heavily on it as though he were a battle hardened soldier in Vietnam who had just single-handedly napalmed yet another village of defenceless Viet Cong.

"Have te knock dese on de head now in de New Year," Mick said, gazing contemptuously at his cigarette.

"Fair play," I muttered. (Wouldn't mind knocking you on the head, you moron.)

"Shouldn't be a problem, it's all in de head really ..." he suggested.

"Yeah," I droned. (Which in your case is your arse.)

I was shooting past the Square at this stage, "disregarding" the amberish-reddish glow of the traffic lights in my haste to get this sap out of my car.

"Dat was a red light yew just went trew dere, my friend," commented Mick.

"No it wasn't," I said defiantly. (What's it to you fucko?)

Mick turned and examined me closely, looking for what exactly I don't know, but a blind man would have seen the absolute contempt I had for him in my steely gaze.

"Where's yer badge?" he inquired sternly.

"There," I said, gesturing towards the dashboard where my badge did indeed lay, though admittedly it was somewhat secreted beneath an array of pens, lighters, chewing gum and cigarettes.

"Dat's not good enough," he chided. "Yer badge is suppost te be on your person at all times. Dat's an offence, dat is," he warned.

"I know it is. The clip's broken, okay?" I replied. (So sue me.)

The clip on my badge had actually broken, and not for the first time either. And it was my third badge as well, I think. The clips on them are not the strongest, and mine had snapped recently, so I had run a paper clip through it and decided to leave it on the dashboard where I could grab it quickly and attach it somehow to my person in the event of being stopped at a checkpoint. Fixing it properly was on my list of things to do, but I hadn't got around to it yet.

"And dis is yew, is it?" Mick then said, pointing at the fare card attached securely to the passenger side of the dashboard, quite remarkably deducing that it should indeed have affixed to it a photograph of me as opposed to Nelson Mandela.

"It is indeed," I replied curtly. (Well done moron, take a bow.)

"I see, I see," Miss Marples continued, "very good. Right so, show me your badge before I get out of the car."

Mick sat back and gave out another jaded sigh before turning around to examine me closely once again.

"What's wrong wit ye? Ye don't seem very happy," he asked.

"I'm tired," I replied wearily. (You're what's wrong with me, moron, now please shut the fuck up annoying me.)

"Yeah well, I don't care if yer tired, cheer up, righ'?" Mick then commanded.

"Ye married?" he continued.

"No." (Fuck off.)

"Kids?"

"No." (Fuck off.)

"Well den?"

"Well then, what?" (Fuck off.)

"Left at the roundabout and straight on 'till I tell you," he instructed.

"Right so."

"Den cheer up, ye've got nuttin to be unhappy about, righ'?"

"Fine." (Fuck off.)

"Yew have no idea what kind o' shit I am goin' inte here now – next left – yew have no idea. If anyone should be unhappy, it's me, but I'm not, see?" Mick said, confusing me altogether, as he was – apart from being the biggest asshole I had met in about six months – quite possibly the single most unhappy person I had met in the same six months. The only thing, or things, that kept him in any way balanced, I suspected, were the chips he carried around on his shoulders, fastened, as they were, to his person by the epaulettes on his leathers, and each representing an area roughly the size of Ghana.

"I see," I said. (Did I ask you to get married to some cow who has come to be a source of angst and frustration for you? Or who, more likely, regrets with every passing day the moment she set eyes on you, and if she could, would give her left leg to turn back the clock and sensibly refuse your request of marriage. No I didn't, so fuck off.)

"Stop de car, pleaze," he said, as though I had just said something incredibly hurtful to him and he had to get out lest I see him cry.

"Now, that's €10.50 please."

"Will ye settle fer a tenner?" he asked extraordinarily.

"What?" I asked, incredulous at his gumption, when in my mind, an altogether fairer proposition would have been if he had given me fourteen thousand euro and the keys to his poxy motorbike so I could sell it and start intensive one-on-one sessions with my therapist – instead of the group ones which I found I didn't really get anything out of – and try to repair the irreparable damage he had done to my head during the past fifteen minutes.

"Will ye settle for a tenner?" he repeated, dead seriously.

"The fare is €10.50," I repeated. (Did you look for a discount on each of the pints you had down in the boozer, you sap?)

"I realise dat, my friend, but I only have a tenner left on me," Mick said.

"Do you? Well give it to me so, and get out." (Don't ever call me friend again, asshole. If us becoming friends could avert the outbreak of nuclear war, I would rather be strapped to the plutonium-filled warhead of the first missile to be launched.)

Mick handed me the tenner in silence. I took it, mumbling the faintest "thank-you", so I could maintain a clean sheet of civility in the verbal exchange I just had to endure. He nodded slowly to himself and got out of the car. Before the door had even closed, I was off down the road to turn around. As I passed his house, he was standing on the footpath, looking intently at me. I was about to give him the finger when I realised he had left his helmet on the back seat. I was momentarily intoxicated with the thought of driving off and throwing the helmet in the canal at Harold's Cross, relishing the delightfully sonorous plop it would make as it broke the sludgy water's surface, but managed to sober up just in time. Instead, I drove on a little further and reached into the back to grab the forgotten item. I stopped the car, opened the door and dropped the helmet unceremoniously on the ground. I then turned towards the rapidly and angrily approaching Mick, extended my forefinger in the manner I had intended to, and drove off quickly, chanting quietly to myself as I went in order to regain my composure.

The S.M.B.W.I.T.W.

Luck is everything in this game really. Well, chance more than luck I suppose, in that the first fare you get every night basically sets in motion a sequence of events that determines every other fare you get that night, be they enjoyable, agonising or utterly despair-inducing. For example, you get a fare to Swords at ten on a Friday night and you're going mad because it takes you completely out of the loop. But then you drop off in whatever estate and as you make your way back through the village, a group of people just happen to be leaving the pub at that exact moment and want to head into town, and you're smiling again, wishing the very best to that bastard-who's-not-a-bastard-anymore who dragged you out to Swords in the first place. Then again, you could get a fare out to Swords at ten on a Friday night and, as before, you're going mad because it takes you completely out of the loop. You drop off there and in the village you get another fare but this time the bastard is going out to the arse end of Donabate or Rush or somewhere, and to top it all, you get a puncture on the way back down some bog road, and you nearly lose your mind cursing the bastard who brought you out to

Swords in the first place. That kind of thing.

So it's a game of chance really, this taxi driving lark, you never really know how or why anyone in your car comes to actually end up in your car. The logical follow-on from this deduction would be – to my mind at any rate – that if fate somehow, sometime, throws you a golden opportunity: grab it and run with it for all it's worth.

It was a wet, cold Thursday night and I had started work unusually early, about five, I suppose. I had been in town in the afternoon and thought I'd get home to have some dinner and wait for the traffic to ease off, but, as is the nature of the beast, I stopped for a guy on the outbound side of Leeson Street who I thought might be heading for somewhere relatively handy like Stillorgan and I could shoot up the bus lane all the way, but no, he wanted to go to Castleknock, of all bloody places. Cursing myself for stopping, and then him for living in poxy Castleknock, I let out a first rate sigh, regretfully made a world-weary U-turn and proceeded to inch my way along the green and then onto Cuffe Street, Kevin Street, Bride Street, Bride Road, Nicholas Street, High Street, Bridge Street Upper and bloody Bridge Street Lower before I could get finally into a bloody bus lane. And then there was a poxy bus in it, thus rendering it useless. Up through the bloody park and after what seemed like seven hours, finally arrived in Laurel Lodge. Emotionally drained and stressed out at being stressed out, I went into the nearest petrol station I could find and bought some gloriously fattening comfort food and sat in the forecourt munching away for a while until I felt able to face the world again.

And so began a fairly uneventful and wholly unenjoyable night's work. But then at about one in the morning, things took a turn for the better. Coming back from Islandbridge, I was shooting down the quays and deliberately broke the lights at

Capel Street, figuring that it was the least I was entitled to do after having been the victim of Dublin's pathetically planned and managed infrastructure for most of the preceding evening. I slowed down as I hit The Morrison just in case there were, (a) any punters around, or (b), and less importantly, any coppers lurking around the new bridge who might see fit to bust me for doing fifty in a thirty. And there they were – a, that is, not b – two absolutely gorgeous girls tottering tipsily out of the hotel. Tall, slim, elegant chicks, absolutely killer bodies with my-daddy-has-a-front-line-apartment-in-Puerto-Banus tans, ass-defining tight faded jeans and sexy sheer loose white frilly blouses. And they were looking for a taxi. *My* taxi. *And* they had their arms raised in the correct fashion. Naturally, I stopped. Very quickly.

"Hi, ohmiGod, thank you *so* much for stopping," said this really gorgeous girl, somewhat breathlessly, as if she couldn't have faced waiting any longer than thirty seconds for a taxi.

"You're welcome," I said casually.

"We love you, Mr Taximan," said the second most beautiful woman in the world, joining her friend in the back seat.

(Now normally I don't have much time for people who address me as Mr Taximan, however genial a tone they might adopt when making such an address, but I was willing to make an exception for this particular client, principally on the grounds that she was, you may have gathered from the title conferred on her in the paragraph above, absolutely gorgeous.)

"Oh yeah?" I said to her smiling. "Cool."

"We're a little bit drunk," she said, smiling mischievously as she made a teensy-weensy type gesture with her thumb and forefinger, both of which I had an overwhelming desire to lick.

"That's allowed. Where're you off to?" I asked politely.

"How about your place?" Go on, say it baby, say it, you know you want to. Restraint got the better of her though.

"Paula's off to Sandymount," said the second most beautiful woman in the world, gesturing towards her more drunken girlfriend who by now had slumped a little ungraciously against the side door and was mumbling away to herself, "and then I'm off to Cabinteely."

"No problem. Whereabouts in Sandymount do you want?" I asked, taking off down the quays.

"I'm on the coast road please," Paula said quietly.

"Right so," I said, briefly mapping out the journey in my head. "Was there something on in The Morrison tonight?"

"Yeah, there was a kind of a launch thing on," said the S.M.B.W.I.T.W. casually, as if attending such launches was a by now familiar and somewhat taxing experience. But she said it in a very down to earth way, and I accepted that she was not at all fazed by the glitz and glamour of the Dublin Z list celebrity circuit. So anyway, I whip down City Quay, on to Pearse Street and on out through Irishtown on to the strand road, all the time chatting away goodo to the S.M.B.W.I.T.W. and it turns out that she's quite cool as well. Shakes her booty at a few fashion shoots every now and then to pay her way through college, where she's studying pharmacy if you don't mind. From the *country* as well it turns out, though there's no sign of an accent. Very grounded really for such a foxy girl, when so many others not as cute as her at all have their heads totally up their own arse about how great they are. Paula isn't contributing much, except for the odd hiccup here and there. She winds down the window to get some fresh air, and I am suddenly a little uneasy, hoping she doesn't get sick, 'cos that would totally ruin the cool vibe I have going with the S.M.B.W.I.T.W., and as I have discussed in another chapter, the one thing I absolutely will not tolerate in my car is puking, regardless of whether or not the puker is a very close friend of the S.M.B.W.I.T.W. and we happen to be getting along great. Could have a delicate situation here I thought to myself, so I tore along the pleasantly deserted strand road until I was told to stop outside Paula's house. I stood on the brakes and waited impatiently for her to get out. Her egress was somewhat laboured, slowed down as it was by the copious amounts of air kisses that passed between her and the S.M.B.W.I.T.W. Eventually she is gone and as I take off again, the S.M.B.W.I.T.W. decides to join me up front and clambers from back seat to front seat in a terribly undignified, and totally cool, fashion. She settles in and gives me a cheeky smile as I rattle over the tracks at Merrion Gates.

(Obviously at this stage of the proceedings, I knew this girl's name, and she knew mine – my *real* name too – but I am not telling you what it is. Nor am I going to use a fake name – as I have had to do in all of the other stories for legal reasons – because it just wouldn't be the same. Part of what made the S.M.B.W.I.T.W. actually be the S.M.B.W.I.T.W. was her name; at least that was part of it for me. You hear some people say, "What's in a name?" dismissively, as if there wasn't, in fact, much to a person's name. That's horseshit; everything is in a name. *The* most beautiful woman in the world at *any* time, past, present or in the future, happens to be a girl I went out with for a regrettably very brief period about two years ago, and a huge part of what made her *the* most beautiful woman in the world was her name. I have never met anyone else with the same name, and nor do I want to. It was so unique, and suited her perfectly. And no, I am not going to tell you what her name was either. Physically, she wasn't actually my "type", if I can say such a thing without sounding like an arrogant swine, in that she was blond – naturally, as opposed to chemically, and had a rather pale complexion – and I am normally more attracted to dark-skinned brunettes. Undoubtedly attractive as she was, however, when she told me her name she became extraordinarily attractive and I was totally smitten, and after seeing her only twice would have quite happily married her, giving me good reason to repeat her name over and over every day, as opposed to just repeating it over and over anyway as I walked down the street, thereby running the risk of being committed to a mental institution.)

So anyway, we continue on our journey, yakking away to each other, talking the kind of shite you can normally only discuss with someone you've known for ages. Then, as I was driving along the Clonkeen Road, things moved up a notch.

"This is great, isn't it?" she asked.

"What's great?" I in turn asked.

"This. This like," she said, gesturing to and fro with her hands, obviously referring to the warm and fuzzy feeling that filled the car as our twenty-minute old relationship blossomed. "You know, just meeting someone and getting on cool with them from the start like, yeah?"

"Yeah, you're right, it's cool," I agreed. "Most people I get in this car are complete assholes and just piss me off," I continued.

"Oh my God yeah, I'd say you meet some serious morons on your travels," she said laughing. "Where are we now?" she then enquired, looking out the window on to the dark, almost abandoned road.

"Just coming up to Cornelscourt, why?"

"I'd love a drink. I thought I was pissed when I left the hotel, but I feel absolutely fine … Is there anywhere open around here now?"

"What time is it? God no, the only place open now is Club 92," I said nearly disdainfully, as if reckoning she'd no more have any interest in going up there.

"Oh yeah! Club 92! My God, I haven't been up there in ages! Will we go? It's so tragic … it'll be a laugh, yeah, let's!"

"Yeah, okay, cool," I said quickly, for once not looking a gift horse in the mouth.

Sixteen seconds later the car was parked and the S.M.B.W.I.T.W. and I were walking hand in hand towards the club of love, as it is rather optimistically – and on this occasion, rather fittingly, I hoped – called. She then stopped suddenly and turned to me.

"Hey, do you know what?"

"What?" I replied, because I didn't.

"You know the way we're getting on really well an' all?"

"Yeah ... so?"

"So I don't want it to be awkward later on like, when I'm going home ... and you might want, to snog me, or I might want to snog you and, it'd be really awkward so, let's ... let's just have a little snog now and get it out of the way, yeah? Then there'll be no big build up to anything and ..."

And with that, the S.M.B.W.I.T.W. – who happened to have a very fine insight into the workings of the human mind – leaned over, put arms around my neck and we started snogging. Big time. And it was totally cool, full on tonsil action. We fooled around for a while in as shameful a manner as our all too public location would permit, and then progressed inside.

I got two beers and joined the S.M.B.W.I.T.W. at a table she had managed to secure. Tunes were fairly crap and the place was indeed tragic, full of assholes, a good number of whom were wage slaves in their office attire. Then the S.M.B.W.I.T.W. wanted to dance. This is where things could have gotten rocky. I don't dance, never have, never will, principally because I can't, and as a general rule of thumb, I try to avoid knowingly making a tit of myself. (In all reality, *most* people can't dance, but the scary thing is, this knowledge doesn't in itself stop them from dancing, something which I find overwhelmingly disturbing.) I smile and politely decline the invitation, and independent free spirit that she is, the S.M.B.W.I.T.W. gets up and goes for a boogie herself. I watch as she shakes her ass on the dance floor, and sure enough, she's a great dancer as well. All that posturing on the catwalk pays dividends I suppose. I sip my beer and happily drool in her direction for a few minutes as she smiles and gives me a wave every now and then. After a while, nature calls and I go to relieve myself. When I get back and retake my seat, I see her again, the S.M.B.W.I.T.W., still dancing away happily, only this time she kind of has her arms around one of those wage slaves, who is wearing – I kid you not – a navy suit, white shirt and a *red* tie! He looks like some loser wannabe stock broker from a documentary taking a nostalgic look back at the heady days of the late eighties bull market in London. As I ponder the scene before me, she looks over and waves, smiling cringingly as she does so. The slow song ends and she smiles gratefully at the guy and joins me once again.

"Oh *my* God, what a saddo! Where did you get to?" she asked me, seeming somewhat upset that I had deserted her.

"The little boy's room," I replied. "How was your dance?"

"Tragic," she said, raising her big dark eyes heavenward. "He kept moving over towards me, and then before I knew it, he had his arms around me when that song came on ... Jesus ... I need a drink. You want another beer?"

"No thanks, better not. You get one if you want, it's cool," I replied.

"Maybe I shouldn't really, actually feel quite pissed now ... What time is it anyway?"

"Ah, just gone half two," I said, checking the clock on my phone.

"Shit, is it? I better head home, I suppose ..."

"Yeah cool, c'mon so, I'll drop you up."

"Thanks a million," she said smiling.

"No problem, let's go."

And so we left the club of love and returned to my taxi, got in and headed, after a wholly unexpected and utterly delightful diversion, to Cabinteely, where I dropped the S.M.B.W.I.T.W. off at her house. She gave me a kiss on the cheek, thanked me for the lift and the beer, got out and skipped up the steps to her duplex apartment. As I headed back down the dualler in the general direction of town, I figured that this particular night was not going to get any better and I too decided to go home to bed.

In de hite of it

oming back along the Cromwellsfort Road one evening
on one of the off-peak nights during last Christmas. (I say
off-peak nights in that it wasn't Christmas Eve or New
Year's Eve, more like the twenty-eighth or twenty-ninth,
something like that, though collectively, the whole Christmas
period, even if supposed to be extremely manic, was in fact –
thanks largely to Mr McCreevey's abhorrent mismanagement of
the greatest period of economic growth this banana republic has
ever witnessed – decidedly off-peak in its entirety, and not very
busy at all.) This bird moves along the road ahead of a few
punters and waves me down. I saw what she was up to alright,
skipping the queue – if a disparate grouping of people in various
states of inebriation loosely assembled around a busy junction
can be called a queue – but it's nothing to do with me, so I pull in
and she trots excitedly towards the car, shouting frantically at her
cohort across the road, who had obviously been trying the same
trick on the opposite side of the road in the hope of snaring an
empty outbound taxi.

"Brian, wud ye c'mon! I got one!" she shrieked victoriously.

"Deadly! Ye good ting ye!" Brian congratulated her as he jayran across the road.

"How's it going? Where are we off to?" I asked.

"We're goin' te Clondalkin te get, ah … te get someone, an' den back here, is dat alrigh?" inquires the illegally blonde in the back.

"Yeah, that's grand," I replied casually, delighted that I had bagged a return fare.

As I pulled a U-turn, another couple moved up towards the hot spot where this bird had bagged me, the male of the pairing quite irate at having had his position in the "queue" usurped.

"Dat's our bleedin' taxi, yis wankers!" he roared at the usurpers, somehow under the impression that the only reason I had for driving down that particular road at that exact time was to expressly collect him and his other half.

"Ha, ha, fuck youse, we god a taxi and youse don't!" Brian shouted childishly out the window, waving at the usurpees as we turned around.

"Whereabouts in Clondalkin do you want?" I asked, as if I knew every inch of it by heart.

"We're goin' te St John's, d'ye know it?" she asked, "it's behind de Green Isle, yeah?" she then said, helpfully answering her own question.

"I do, yeah, that's grand," I lied.

I hadn't known it, but now I did, and headed up through Ballymount to get out on to the Naas Road, listening as Brian and blondie hatched their plan.

"Louise, lissen te me yeah," he instructed. "Yew ring dis lad an' have 'im meet is, righ?"

"Yeah I will, relax de kax, he's kool, alrigh'?" Louise replied, taking out her mobile.

"Howiya doin' bud, ye well?" says Brian, politely enquiring

after my general health and well-being.

"Yeah I'm grand," I answered, feeling comparatively loquacious. "How're things with you?"

"Deadly buzz man, yeah, deadly. In de pub dere wit de gang from work like, Christmas party an' alldat, ye know?"

"Oh yeah? Looking after you well I hope, are they?"

"Yes dey are. Yes dey are indeed, fair play, has te be said. Job issen up te much like, but der're all sound, make sure ye get rightly pissed at dese dos like ..."

"Lissen Mick, we're on our way up now alrigh'? Yeah, we're in a bleedin' joe maxi, bombin' down de Naas Road," I heard Louise remark on the phone.

"Righ', I'll call ye wen we get te de skewel, yeah? An' yew can come around an' meet is, yeah? Righ', kool, bye."

I was heading towards the filter lane at Newlands Cross and noticed Brian looking around at the seemingly unfamiliar surroundings.

"Wear de fuck are we Louise? Are we still in bleedin' Dublin or what?"

"'Course we're in bleedin' Dublin! We're on de Naas Road ye sap!"

"Alrigh', alrigh', kool de jets, I'm owney askin', jus' seen signs fer bleedin' Limerick and Cork dere. D'yew *live* out here, do ye?"

"Yeah, I do, an' it's deadly id is too," said Louise as I turned right at the lights, past the ever-expanding Bewley's hotel.

"Nah, wooden do fer me," Brian decided, shaking his head solemnly. "Sure yer miles from antin. Town's wear it's at now, in all fairness, everyting on yer doorstep, shops, boozers, de lot," he continued, sounding like a spokesperson for the Dublin Docklands Development Authority.

"No way, it's kool out here, I know lodes o' people out here, an' dey all live nearby like, it's great ..."

"But like, how do ye get anywear, d'yew drive in te work, d'ye?"

"'Course I do. Owney takes me about twenty-five minits … yer next left at the lites an' den around towards de Green Isle, yeah?" Louise informs me.

"Grand yeah, no problem," I replied.

"Are we nearly dere Louise?"

"Yeah we are, I'll ged on de fone te Mick now an' tell 'im te come an' meet is."

Brian was obviously a stranger to these parts, and I had therefore dropped the possibility of his being Louise's boyfriend, but she did appear to be playing a critical role in his liaising with this Mick character, and seeing as how they were going back to The Submarine afterwards, I – perhaps somewhat hastily and unfairly – concluded that Mick's role in all of this was that of a drug dealer, a hunch which was confirmed a few moments later by Louise's telephone call.

"Wear are ye now Mick?" she asked. "Yeah, kool, kool, an' how much d'ye want fer it? Righ', yeah, all righ' den, see ye at de shops in a few minits, bye."

"Is it kool Louise, yeah?" enquired Brian casually.

"Yer sekind rite an den all de way down, tanks, yeah id is, don't worry, Mick's sound 'e is," Louise replied.

I proceeded as directed through the estate, more or less remembering my way from previous trips here. I couldn't be arsed necessarily remembering the names of different estates, preferring to rely instead on my rather intuitive sense of direction. Straight down, left, second right, and right again and the aforementioned rendezvous came into sight.

"This where you want, yeah?" I checked.

"Yeah, jus' pull in here fer a minit tanks, he won't be long," reassured Louise.

Didn't bother me how long he was really, I decided to myself as I pulled into the deserted car park at the shops, wasn't that busy out yet and the meter was ticking away nicely. Time is money as they say. I swung around so as to be ready for the off and came to a halt under a lamp post, leaving the engine running and turning up the volume on the CD. (Red Hot Chilli Peppers "By the Way" if you're interested, by the way. Cracking album it is too.)

Louise did what any self-respecting woman does when she has time to kill – attended to make up and hair. Brian asked her for a smoke and she replied that she had left them on the table in the pub. He tut-tutted and shook his head ruefully. I was lighting one myself and offered him one of mine.

"Whad are dey?" he enquired.

"Marlboro Lights," I answered.

"Nah, cudden be doin' wit dem tanks," he said, turning down my offer. "Shite it anyway! Dere must be about two hundred blue on dat poxy table!" he complained.

Rather ironic really, don't you think? Brian spurns my kind offer of a Marlboro Light, pining for his forgotten John Player Blue, when the reason he had left the table on which the preferred cigarettes lay in the first place was to procure an altogether more dangerous substance. I wouldn't have thought that somebody about to ingest contraband narcotics would be that picky about the brand of cigarettes they smoked, but there you go, funny old world.

"Wear ye watchin' de game bud?" Brian continues, changing the subject to distract himself from matters nicotine.

"No, I didn't catch it," I replied, not even knowing what sport he may have been referring to, but reckoning that it was bound to be the UK premiership. "Any good was it?"

"Bleedin' rapit id was man! Bet Man City three two, great

result. I'm a Spurs man meself like, an' ye wanna have seen it up in de sub, all de City heads in deir jerseys! I didden wear mine in case we were goin' on somewear afterwards like, ye know yerself what bleein' bouncers are like, but wen I saw all dem in jerseys? Jaysus, I was in de hite of it den I kin tell ye! Ragin' I was, I wood have luven te have id on me, sicken dem all, de shower o' wankers!" Brain said passionately.

"Any sign of dis bloke Louise?" he said after a minute's gazing out the window.

"Relax, he'll be here in a minit, he's in 'is ma's gaf ..."

"An' wear does she live? Bleedin' Galway? We're here ages fer fuck's sake ..."

"She jus' lives over dem railings, he said he has te ... that'll be him now," Louise said, reaching for her ringing mobile phone.

"Hello? Yeah Mick, kool ... wear are ye now? Yer what? Righ', we'll come on out te ye, bye ... bye, bye."

"Can we jus' go on oud o' here a bit?" she asks me. "He's just walkin' around now like ..."

"Yeah, no problem," I said co-operatively, moving off out of the car park. As I got to the gate however, a lone male came trotting towards the car, nodding his head in a long and slow fashion, as if reciprocating our coded signal. I stopped once again, and looked on as Brian fished a wad of cash out of his pockets.

"Here ye are Louise, yew sort id out wid 'im, yeah? Yew know 'im like," Brian suggested, handing a few notes back to Louise in the back seat.

"Yeah righ', fine," Louise agreed. "Howiya Mick? Alrigh' love, yeah?" she then enquired of Mick as she opened the door.

"Ah yeah, not bad like," Mick replied, taking a moment to scan the car's occupants quickly to make sure he wasn't being entrapped in a sting operation. Visually satisfied with our bona fides, "the deal went down". Louise handed the little package to

Brian for approval before parting with the cash. He gave it what to my mind was a very cursory examination, weighing it up and down in his hand, as if there was a minute electronic weighing scales embedded in his palm. But then again, maybe you do get a feel for these things as you make progress with your drugs dependency. Either way, Brian nodded his head solemnly like The Man From Del Monte did all those years ago, and Louise handed over the little roll of cash. Mick was more thorough in his examination of what he was getting out of the deal, and unfurled the roll to count the money, mouthing silently as he did so. Judging from his strained eyes and lethargic movements, I suspected that Mick was an avid, and very recent, consumer of the product he also wholesaled. All tallies and inventories complete, customer and broker bade farewell to supplier and we set off for the return leg of the journey. Brian secreted the package carefully in the tiny little pocket above the main right pocket of his jeans, patting it gently when he was done.

I tore back through the estate and got on to the Naas Road, heading back to our destination. As I drove, Louise pointed towards a row of houses around a green and prodded Brian's shoulder.

"See dem houses dere Brian? Dat's wear dose kids lived, d'ye 'member de ones I was tellin' ye about dat got kilt in de car down be de canal?" she said.

"Oh yeah? Two brudders wassen it? Dey robbed some car and ..."

"Yeah, an' dey had anudder lad in it wit dem, tree o' dem dere was. An' dey wear bombin' down de canal an' swerved te avoid dese auld ones crossin' de road an' ended up in de canal. De two brudders were kilt, but de udder young fella managed te ged out ..." Louise explained.

"Dese are de tings dat happen Louise, dese are de tings dat

happen wen ye do tings like dat," Brian surmised, again somewhat ironically I thought to myself. He was obviously able to rationalise and distinguish, in his own mind at least, the difference between the insanity of robbing a car for a joyride and ending up dead in the Grand Canal and habitually using drugs for recreational purposes, when he himself could possibly, at some stage in the future, end up dead in the same Canal as a result of his involvement with underworld figures. I figured it was best to keep my observations to myself, hoping that Brian was only an infrequent user and would sooner or later knock his habit on the head altogether.

"I know, I know. It's very sad but, all de same," concluded Louise quietly.

"Id is yeah, id surely is," agreed Brian, and then changing the subject to more pressing matters, "here, what time is it?"

"Half ten," answered Louise, "here, d'ye reckin dey'll all go on to a club after?"

"Oh yes dey will, def-a-bleedin'-itely. Yew goin are ye?"

"Fuckin' rite I'm goin!" Louise replied emphatically. "Wear'll we go?"

"I don't mind, I jus' wanna ged off me face," said Brian, echoing the sentiments of the vast majority of people out and about that night.

The rules of attraction

The old Volvo died on me, God love her. Eleven years service under her belt. And that was what did it as well, ironically. The timing belt went on her one Saturday night when I was out in Killiney. Had just dropped people off in the Court hotel and was coming out of the car park when she gave up. Not that I knew it was the timing belt; it was the AA man who told me that. Luckily enough though, I had the previous week purchased a Saab 9000 from a huckster culchie car dealer I had met in the car one Sunday night, so after a week of toing and froing between insurers, Dublin City Council and the NCTS, I was back on the road. Sad to say goodbye to the old Volvo though, you really can't beat them if you want a good old workhorse. Go forever they will if you look after them. I hadn't actually had that one for too long myself, got it from the brother-in-law when he was changing up. She was a '91 reg and he'd driven her from about '92 onwards, clocking up 279,000 miles on her by the time I took over at the helm, and I got her to 318,000 comfortably. The timing belt going was a portent of things to come; I reckoned the suspension was next to go, and it wasn't worth spending the money on her, so I got her down to a Volvo graveyard in Wexford and parted company with her. And now, as I said, I'm in a Saab, and very happy I am with her as well. I was looking for another Volvo, but couldn't find an automatic one I liked, so I settled on the Saab.

The preceding short history of my vehicular partners does serve a purpose. Compared to most people, I spend a disproportionate amount of my time in my car, anything from fifty-five to seventy hours a week in fact. Consequently, it's important to me that I like the car I drive, and that we get on well together. Some taxi lads will drive any old piece of shit Jap import Corolla into the ground and not give a shite about it, but not me. I respect my cars big time. Not only are they a source of mobility, getting me from A to B safely and protected from the elements, but in my current occupation, are also obviously instrumental in providing me with an income. The relationship between me and my car grows and strengthens every week as I clock up another thousand miles or so, and is currently the only serious relationship I am involved in.

Were I looking for an animate partner with whom to drive down love's long highway, a relaxed compatibility with the prospective candidate would be a prerequisite. Sounds fairly obvious I hear you say, and yes, you would think it is. But why is it then that so many people end up in relationships with people to whom they are entirely ill suited? I'm sure you'll agree that the contents of some of the chapters of this book candidly illustrate how mismatched some couples are. If that in itself wasn't cause for concern on a societal level, the terrifying thing is that many of these relationships actually seem to positively thrive on the, to my mind, rather extreme *frisson* that this mismatch of likes and dislikes causes. Absolutely baffles me to be honest with you. Ladies, if you're interested (though after finishing this book, you more than likely will not be, given the light it portrays me in), in my opinion, shared flaws and qualities are essential in soul mates, as is a jaded and cynical but at the same time decidedly optimistic outlook on life. A little diversity of character is dandy obviously, but there has to be a lot of common ground in the first place, otherwise it's nothing but drama, constant bickering and disagreement over stupid things that don't amount to a hill of beans, and quite frankly would not be the most reassuring indicator of how you would deal with a genuinely serious crisis in your relationship. So please, if you're one of those women who has ever said, "But making up was great," to your girlfriends after regurgitating every last detail of yet another bust-up with your partner over some trivial matter, then you need not apply for the currently vacant position of my girlfriend.

This brings me rather neatly, I think, to my next little tale, concerning itself as it does with an observation of the above mentioned and derided *frisson* at work between what was, to my mind, a wholly mismatched couple.

Half eight, nine o'clock on a Saturday night found me cruising around looking for a fare. I was going up Leeson Street, heading for Donnybrook, when a guy on the bridge flagged me down. I pull in as best I can in the awkward spot, and he and his partner climb in the back.

"Keogh's, please," he says to me politely.

"Right so," I said, somewhat disappointed at the brevity of the fare ahead of me. Managed to pull a quick U-turn and headed back down Leeson Street for the couple of hundred yards journey to Dawson Street. The pair in the back resumed their conversation.

"Yeah, I said we'd meet up in Keogh's for a drink first, the restaurant's only around the corner. Stevie loves the old traditional pubs ... he's a *gaelgór*, did you know that?" he says to his girlfriend.

"No! Is he really? Wow, that's great ... I'm fluent in Irish as well," she contributed.

Your man seemed a bit taken aback at this information, and gave her a strange look.

"You? No you're not ..." he countered.

"Yes I am," she said standing her ground, and then clarifying the position a little, "Well I was ... more or less. Went to the Gaeltacht five years running ..."

"Jesus, that was twenty years ago! I went to the Gaeltacht as well you know, but I wouldn't say I was fluent in Irish, for fuck's sake. You're full of shit do you know that? You said you speak French as well, and you haven't a word of French ..."

"Excuse me, I do so!" she retorted indignantly. "I was an *an pair* for a year and I did French in college ..."

"Yeah, yeah, aren't you great? You still don't speak French though, do you?" your man continued.

"I *do* speak French ..." she protested.

Then your man started rattling on in French. Now I did French at school and was fairly handy at it too, but whatever smattering of the language I had is very rusty, so I wouldn't claim to be able to speak it *per se*, but your one, for all her *au pair*-ing and third level French, was totally lost after about twenty seconds. She was obviously self-delusional, somehow thinking that all she had to do was merely reside for a time in a particular area and she would automatically be imbued with the vernacular.

"Oh do shut up!" she implored irritably. "I can acquit myself quite capably whenever I'm in France ..."

"Fine, that's absolutely fine, fair play to you, but it's not the same thing is it? And now you're after saying you speak Irish, so I'm gonna tell Stevie that's what you said and drop you right in it with him ..."

"Don't be such as asshole Adrian, okay? All I said was ..."

"Oh relax, would you, I'm only messing. Come here," said Adrian (Adrian? What a name! It's a girl's name isn't it?), pulling his girlfriend close for a reconciliatory hug.

The accord reached was not to last for long, however. As we crossed Leeson Street on to the green, Adrian – the boy with the girl's name – recognised the song on the radio.

"Oh, great tune. Turn that up will you?" he asked me.

I obliged happily, for it was indeed a great tune – "Get Free" – from a great band, The Vines.

Adrian starts to rock out in the back as only a middle-aged man with a girl's name can – sadly. His girlfriend, who probably knew the song as well but was a little rusty on its provenance, cops on eventually and starts rocking too.

"They're cool aren't they?" she asks Adrian.

"Yeah, brilliant," he agrees, then adding, "they're from Australia," as if it was somehow breaking the mould for a cool band to originate from that part of the world. This information though proves to be a bone of contention for his erstwhile girlfriend.

"The Devines? No, they're not, they're ..." she says quickly and assuredly.

"Yes they fucking are," he says, "and they're not called The Devines, it's ..."

"They *are* The Devines, okay? Why do you disagree with everything I say? Jesus ..."

"Because you're fucking wrong, that's why!" he replied logically. "They're called The, Vines, okay? *Not*, The, Devines. The, Vines, and they're from Australia."

"I don't think so," she said, standing her rapidly softening ground.

I knew what was going to happen next – I was going to be called upon to act as mediator, validating one party's case and destroying another's.

"Excuse me, Mr Taximan?" Adrian says. (Look up Taximan in the phone book and see how many there are by the way. None.) "Could you please tell *her* the name of this band?"

"The Vines," I said, intonating clearly.

"See?" Adrian snorted triumphantly. "Told you. The, Vines."

"Alright, so I heard it wrong, big deal," the girlfriend said capitulating, "but they're English, not Australian ..."

"Excuse me Mr Taximan? Where are The, Vines from?" Adrian asked, directing the question at me whilst looking smugly at his girlfriend.

"Australia," I replied tersely, somewhat annoyed at seeming to be supporting the boy-girl, when all I was doing was confirming the geographical origin of the band in question.

"See?" Adrian said brusquely, gesturing towards me with his hand as if I were some kind of demi-god oracle type figure.

"What does he know?" she countered with, instantly shattering my only recently conferred demi-god oracle type status.

"Oh for fuck's sake Marian, don't be such a baby. I'm right and you're wrong. That's all there is to it," Adrian said sportingly as I pulled in to the kerb at the corner of South Anne Street.

I tallied the meter, half expecting them to argue over who was going to pay the fare, but thankfully no, Adrian pulled out a load of change and settled up promptly.

"There you go, that's fine, keep the change, thanks," he said.

"Cool, thanks a lot," I said gratefully. Whatever about being an argumentative bastard, his gratuity percentages were spot on.

"You right?" he said, turning to Marian. "What time did your sister say she'd be in at?"

"Oh she's gonna meet us in the restaurant, said it'd probably be nine by the time she got in, so she said she'd go straight ..."

"Why? Table's booked for half, not nine," said Adrian to Marian as he opened the door.

"What? You told me it was nine!" shrieked Marian.

"No I didn't, I said I *tried* to get it for nine but all they could do was half. Why do you think we're going for a drink first?" explained Adrian as he held the door open for Marian to get out.

"Oh for fuck's sake Adrian, now I have to ring Gráinne and ..." Marian complained.

"Thanks, all the best," Adrian said to me, raising his eyes to heaven as he turned to join Marian. "Don't start that moany shit with me. If you listened to what I said in the first ..."

Adrian's voice tailed off as he closed the door and followed Marian towards Keogh's.

Unbelievable. In the space of a quarter of a mile, this couple had argued over Marian's economy with the truth when claiming she could speak both French and Irish, the name and origin of one of the most talked about up-and-coming rock bands, and the exact time Adrian said he had booked the restaurant for. And all in the space of seven or eight minutes. Now I'm sorry, but that is not what I would call a healthy, balanced and sustainable relationship.

But then again, I'm single, so what the hell would I know?

Epilogue

Well, I had a prologue, so I'm gonna have me an epilogue too. Kind of bookends the whole undertaking, if you'll pardon the pun, which is fully intended. I have to say that as I scan the pages of this thankfully completed book, I am finally convinced that I really don't want to be a taxi driver anymore. I am just not cut out for it, I think. (Not in an operational sense obviously; I'm a highly competent driver and I know my way around this city backwards.) It's because driving a taxi exposes me to the kind of shit I don't want to see. At least not anymore. I've seen and learnt a lot from my time as a public service vehicle driver. That's probably the biggest thing I've gotten out of this whole taxi driving lark really, to be honest – just seeing stuff. (Sure, I've made a living, but I would have made that elsewhere if not on the streets of Dublin.) Taxi driving has copped me on a lot; I saw a lot of life, however much I didn't want to see it at the time, but would now like to think that I am a more rounded individual as a result of the quarter of a million miles or so I have put on the clocks of my various cars. A lot of people, given the choice, would rather avoid seeing the underbelly of their immediate surroundings so closely, and maybe they're right as well. But that's what I did, and I don't regret it.

But now I know Dublin too well, and I don't like the city it has become. And continuing as a taxi driver means I'm only going to get to know it better, and that means I'm going to like it even less, and I don't want that to happen. I know that in practically every story you've read to get to this point, I have a go at it in one way or another. That's partly because I'm a narky, cynical bastard who all too often finds it easier to say something bad about something or someone than to say something nice, or nothing at all, and that's not really a good thing. I've always been like that to a large degree, as my family and handful of friends will quickly attest to, but driving a taxi has definitely made me worse. When you spend sixty hours or more a week driving around a city as small as Dublin, stopping at the side of the road to pick up complete strangers from all walks of life who collectively constitute the DNA of the city, the Bord Fáilte bullshit of the city of a thousand welcomes quickly fades away as the X-ray like facility of driving a taxi in Dublin reveals the real psyche and make up of the people that populate it. And how more accurate a feel for, or understanding of, a city can you get than one for, or of, its people, for what is a city without its people?

And in my current position, I only ever see the bad points of this city. I've seen gangs of scumbags around town, knives and coshes secreted about their persons, actually looking for a fight. I've seen kids develop a lifestyle that could well land them in jail before they're sixteen or seventeen, one guy of about fourteen walking up Fitzwilliam Street who spotted a mobile phone in a parked Volvo and instinctively took off his jacket, wrapped it around his fist, smashed the window and made off at only a canter with his swag. I've seen destitute refugees verbally and physically abused and spat at by young girls on O'Connell Street. (What kind of hellish places do they originate from if they perceive Dublin as a better alternative to their homeland?) I've seen little kids out and about at two in the morning when they should have been at home in bed or watching telly with their parents, one young lad who couldn't have been more than eight or nine, passed out on the forecourt of a garage in Dolphin's Barn, twisted drunk on cheap cider. I've seen tourists visiting the Emerald Isle mugged in broad daylight on main thoroughfares as people pass on by. I've seen young girls, really young girls, totally pissed, walking home alone at three in the morning across poorly lit open greens and down dark lanes, some of whom don't make it home. I've seen people who would consider themselves to be pillars of the community quicken their pace as they walk past homeless people in doorways, as if poverty and social exclusion were diseases that travelled through the air. I could go on and on and on, but I won't, because it won't make any difference. Now I know there's a lot of good people out there as well, genuinely decent people who do try and do their bit to help their fellow man, and I'd like to think that sometimes I am among their number. But then a lot of the time, I know I'm not, and doing nothing about something bad only perpetuates the cycle.

Worse still, not doing something about the situation I have just lamented basically conjoins me to those people I have just lambasted, in that if I'm not part of the solution I must be part of the problem. And I'm not going to say, "But what can one person do?" because that's bullshit. One person, you, or me could do a lot, but a lot of people could do a lot more. And whilst not wanting to make it look as though I am looking for an excuse to absent myself from doing something, I actually think that most people in Dublin think it's a great spot to live and work, and that there isn't really much wrong with the place. I reckon if I drove them around for a couple of nights, their rose-tinted glasses might become a little clearer, but even then I don't think they'd be too pushed about doing anything about it.

I harbour this fanciful notion of taking myself off to the south of France and buying an old farmhouse on a hill a couple of miles from a small village and living a simple, contented life in relative isolation, and whilst I am fully aware that the south of France, anywhere in France, or indeed anywhere anywhere has its own problems, I still manage to convince myself that I could have a better life there, be more relaxed and at peace, because the problems there are not my doing. I'm Irish, not French; it's nothing to do with me. Move country and obtain instant admonition from the woes of your new domicile. It was like that when I got here, as Homer Simpson would say. Maybe it'll work, maybe not. Or maybe it's just me, and Dublin is, comparatively speaking, actually a great city with many more redeeming qualities than it has negatives. My brother now lives in California and was home for Christmas last year. He had a great time for three weeks, catching up with friends and family, but was delighted to go back. Dublin's a great city to come *back* to, he'd say. The negatives of Dublin are happily absent from his new set up in California. But the few remaining positives of Dublin aren't there either, so it's something of a trade-off. I think I could live with that though.

In my opinion (and that's all it is – my opinion – and it's no more or less valid than yours, or the person's sitting across from you on the DART in the morning, or the van driver's behind you in the traffic on the way home), a big part of the reason Dublin is now such a shithole is the unprecedented level of economic success enjoyed by the country in general, and Dublin in particular. New jobs were being created in new industries at a faster rate than jobs were being lost in more traditional sectors. The corruption-ridden construction trade was rocking, most people were doing well, thought they were laughing and went out and financed a new car or conservatory on the back of the increased equity in their homes, the value of which had doubled or tripled in about five or six years. The propaganda spewn out by spin-doctors and the media led people to believe, or at least made it easier for them to believe, that everything was grand, and that our status as the fastest growing economy in Europe, with bullshit stats the envy of every developed country in the world, would see us through as a nation for years. I reckon, however, that it will actually be our undoing, and that that undoing has started, and that it's going to take something special to undo this undoing.

People have become selfish. I typed lots of different words there before I settled on selfish. I tried assholes, my perennial favourite, but that didn't work. Neither did greedy; or wankers. But a quick reference to the dictionary proved that selfish was actually the most fitting, in that it is an adjective describing a condition where one is "concerned chiefly with one's own personal profit or pleasure at the expense of consideration for others". Less than a centimetre down from that word is self*less*, which describes a condition where one is "concerned more with the needs and wishes of others than one's own". So close, and yet miles apart. And that's what wrong with Dublin. It's a selfish city.

And I'm not talking about all the blatant, pre-meditated criminal goings-on that our under and over world figures get up to, or the politicians who willingly aid and abet them in their avaricious activities. That kind of thing goes on everywhere, and all the rainforest-depleting reports that are the result of the litany of expensive tribunals that are putting serious pressure on the space available in Dublin Castle are not going to change anything really. Nobody's going to end up in jail. Unfortunately. And if one of them did, they'd be out again in a few months, to make space for some petty criminal who slipped through the cracks of the unbalanced society that that same bastard's nefarious dealings have helped to create. No, what I'm talking about are the little things that collectively make a particular place worth living in or not, and that the absence of these little things can ultimately be the ruination of that same place. I was listening to the Pat Kenny show one day early in January of this year when he recounted a story a listener had phoned in with. A woman called Elaine said that her mother was in the village of Dundrum the previous day. An elderly woman, she had recently lost her husband, and was also suffering from Alzheimer's. She was walking home to her house when she suddenly felt unwell, and quite faint. She saw a woman across the road loading up her jeep with shopping bags and approached her to ask her if she would be so good as to give her a lift up the road to her house, a couple of hundred yards away. The woman point blank said no, that she was busy and had to collect her children from school.

I was going to say next that I couldn't believe this had happened, but the reality is that I can all too readily believe that this happened, because this is the city that Dublin has become. Like I said before, you have no control over where, or into what circumstances you are born. I, by virtue of being lucky enough to have been born into a family headed by the two most right-thinking and decent people I know who worked hard to provide a comfortable and secure environment for their family, was born in Dundrum. I remember it as being a place where nothing much happened, peopled by generally decent folk.

I would hate to think that I knew this woman who refused the most simple and least troublesome kindness to an elderly woman who lived in her neighbourhood. I sincerely, genuinely, earnestly, really do hope that some night – preferably tonight – when she is driving her fucking jeep along the Stillorgan dual carriageway in the pissing rain, she gets a blow out, and when she goes to get the spare wheel it is flat, and when she goes to ring her husband her mobile battery dies on her, and she has to stand on the hard shoulder and try to wave down a passing motorist, and when one eventually stops to see what the trouble is, they tell her that they can't help her because they have to get home to watch ER, and she is left stranded there for hours before having to walk home in the pitch dark, in the pissing rain, and she has no jacket and the new clothes she is wearing are utterly destroyed, and her recently coloured hair is dank and lifeless, and her mascara is streaming down her self piteously tear-stained face, and when she gets home she realises she has locked her keys in her jeep and her husband has taken the kids to the cinema, and her neighbours on both sides are out playing bridge, and she collapses in a heap on her doorstep, sobbing deeply as she buries her head in her hands, and wonders, "Why me?" And from somewhere inside her, a voice tells her, "It's because you're a selfish fucking bitch who couldn't bring yourself to do one little thing for an elderly lady who politely asked you for a lift up the fucking road, that's fucking why."

Okay, that's enough I suppose. My overlong, poorly structured, rambling polemic will not change anything. I've had enough. I'm tired. Good luck.